21ST CENTURY WEALTH

21ST CENTURY WEALTH

THE MILLENNIAL'S GUIDE
to Achieving Financial Independence

RACHEL PODNOS O'LEARY

MANJUL
Manjul Publishing House

First published in India by

MANJUL

Manjul Publishing House
•C-16, Sector 3, Noida, Uttar Pradesh 201301 – India
Website: www.manjulindia.com

Registered Office:
•10, Nishat Colony, Bhopal 462 003 – India

Distribution Centres
Ahmedabad, Bengaluru, Bhopal, Kolkata, Chennai,
Hyderabad, Mumbai, New Delhi, Pune

This edition first published in 2024

ISBN 978-93-5543-292-6

Cover design: Sheila Parr

Printed and bound in India by Thomson Press (India) Ltd.

To my husband, Thomas

CONTENTS

INTRODUCTION

My friend Maggie is a millennial, just like you and me. She is a Physician Assistant, married to an environmental lawyer, and they have two young children. They also have the burden of over $300,000 in student loan debt.

Maggie moved to Miami after graduate school, and I made frequent weekend trips to visit her. We had a blast. We were young and single, with no real responsibilities, and we spent those years (and our money) living it up. All the while, the balance of Maggie's student loans was like a dark cloud hanging over her head, just waiting to make her sunny life miserable with reminders of where her money *should* have been going. When monthly statements came in the mail, she'd throw them away unopened, saying, "I don't even want to look at it."

She felt hopeless, like she'd never get out from under her debt. Avoiding it made her feel better, at least for a while. Maggie even installed one of those apps that rounds up every online purchase to the nearest dollar and puts the change into a savings account. The account grew slowly, increasing by pennies, nickels, and dimes. But she would end up spending the savings on clothes or nights out at the bars rather than paying down her loans. Her situation got more unmanageable by the day.

Then Maggie met Greg, an environmental lawyer with a heavy student loan burden of his own. They got married, rented an apartment in Miami together, and had their first child. Although they lived comfortably on two incomes, they didn't put any extra toward their student loans.

Instead, they continued making minimum payments on Greg's debt, while Maggie enrolled in the public service loan forgiveness program (PSLF). Because the hospital where she worked was a nonprofit, she qualified for this program, which required only the smallest of regular monthly payments for ten years, at which point the loans would be forgiven in full. The catch? She had to continue working full-time in an eligible position for the entire duration. The other catch? The minimal monthly payments permitted under PSLF barely covered the interest portion of each payment, meaning that the 7.1-percent interest on her loans would continue to grow the remaining balance larger and larger over that ten-year repayment period.

Then, as it so often does, life came calling.

Greg was offered a job opportunity in Colorado, a dream job (with a dream income) that was too good to pass up. So they uprooted their lives and made the move. Upon arriving in Colorado, Maggie had a difficult time finding a job. Then she and Greg were presented with another surprise: she was pregnant with their second child!

Between these two circumstances, Maggie was out of work for about a year, and no longer qualified for the public service loan forgiveness program. "I'm so screwed," she told me.

In fact, she was more screwed than she thought. Not only would her massive balance no longer be forgiven, but the interest had been accumulating on her loans for *years* while she made minimal payments under the PSLF program. She and Greg actually owed more now than they had when they got married, in addition to a mortgage and two additional mouths to feed.

"What can we *do?*" she asked me on one of our video chats. Even through the screen, I could see the toll the stress was taking on her.

"Well," I began, before she cut me off, blowing her bangs off her forehead with the force of the gigantic sigh she heaved.

"What does it even matter? Making those payments is like dropping grains of sand on the beach."

Their lives, their debt, and their financial future felt out of control.

WHAT WE NEED

Maggie's story is a very specific example, but it illustrates common themes for people of our generation—and, as a millennial financial planner, I hear similar stories *all the time*.

This may not be your exact experience. You may have less debt. You may live somewhere with a lower cost of living. You may come from a different background or have a different career path. Whatever the specifics of your life and your financial situation, we universally face a different landscape than that of the generations that came before us.

Many of us came of age right around the Great Recession, and, as a generation, millennials are still behind. According to the report "The Emerging Millennial Wealth Gap" by nonpartisan think tank New America, millennials make an average of 20 percent less money than our parents' generation did at our age.[1]

---

1 Reid Cramer, Fenaba R. Addo, Colleen Campbell, "The Emerging Millennial Wealth Gap," NewAmerica.com, last updated October 29, 2019, https://www.newamerica.org/millennials/reports/emerging-millennial-wealth-gap/.

We're also under-employed to a much larger degree, regardless of education level. On top of that, many of us are facing massive student loan debt burdens unlike anything ever seen before—a unique, if not defining, trait of our generation.

In pursuit of financial success and stability, many millennials have ended up in the opposite situation. Innocently and optimistically trying to better our lives with the best of intentions, we bought houses because *that*, we were told, *is what you do*. We got graduate degrees because *that's the way to a good life*. We bought cars and spent and borrowed because that is what worked for our parents, our role models, our financial influencers—and now many of us are stuck.

We all have different stories to tell, but at the end of the day, we generally have similar goals. We want to know that we can pay for the things that are important to us. We want the peace of mind that comes from knowing we'll be okay later in life. We want stability, security, and freedom.

I'm here to tell you that there *is* a way for you to have all of that—and more. But it won't necessarily happen by following in your parents' footsteps.

NOT YOUR PARENTS' FINANCIAL PLANNING

We millennials need sound financial advice tailored *specifically for us*.

I'm not writing this book because there aren't any financial planning or wealth management books out there. In fact, there are a ton; it's a hugely popular section of Amazon's listings. Personal finance is not a new subject, but much of the information currently out there isn't aimed at people like me and you. Most of the financial planning and wealth management books out there speak to a baby-boomer-aged (or older) audience.

And that's why I'm writing this book. As both a millennial and a Certified Financial Planner™ (CFP), I'm keenly aware of the unique obstacles millennials face when it comes to building wealth.

Maybe in reaction to the difficult economic climate during which we came of age, some pretty out-there trends have caught on in the millennial personal finance community. One example is the FIRE movement, which stands for Financial Independence, Retire Early. Followers of this movement save a relatively large percentage of their income—as high as 80 percent—for a period of years, in order to achieve financial independence and retire in their thirties and forties. Many FIRE followers go to extreme lengths to hit their savings targets: living in vans, cutting their own hair, eating canned beans, and giving up most, if not all, material comforts.

There's nothing wrong with this approach, but I personally

don't find it very appealing. I'm more of an "everything in moderation" type of person, so extreme lifestyles just don't appeal to me. I enjoy getting my hair professionally styled, dining out, and indulging in life's pleasures here and there. That's why this book isn't going to tell you to cut up all your credit cards and never get another. It's not going to tell you to cut your own hair to save money. I'm also not going to lie to you and say that skipping a latte once a week will lead to riches beyond your wildest dreams.

I wrote this for people like myself—people who don't want to live in vans and life-hack their way to early retirement, but who *do* want to get on the path to financial independence and learn how to build wealth over the long term. The advice in this book is tailored for millennials, people in their late twenties and thirties who have already earned their degrees and begun their careers. They're starting families, buying first homes, juggling student loans, and saving for the future—often all at the same time.

And I know how all of that feels—while writing this book, I got married, bought my first house, and became pregnant with my first child. It's been fun, but it's *a lot*. That's why I focused on making sure that the advice in this book is moderate, reasonable, and actionable. As a busy young person, that's exactly what *I* would want in a financial advice book.

FACING THE FACTS

My goal is to give you practical advice that all of us *should* know—but which most of us don't, not even many of the most educated and highest-earning professionals among us. I can't tell you how many brilliant lawyers, doctors, and entrepreneurs I come across every day who make massive financial mistakes. Unfortunately, many people are forced to learn these lessons the hard way, by suffering the consequences—and paying the literal price.

I'm hoping that reading this book may save you thousands to hundreds of thousands of dollars—and help you avoid making costly financial mistakes that could prevent you from building wealth. I've filled these pages with common-sense advice you probably didn't learn in school and won't hear from the majority of people holding themselves up as so-called "financial advisors."

As Charlie Munger, vice-chairman of Berkshire Hathaway, says, "It is remarkable how much long-term advantage people like us have gotten by trying to be consistently not stupid, instead of trying to be very intelligent."

You may not know what kind of retirement plan you have—or whether your employer even offers one. If you do have one, you may not know how much you're contributing or whether it comes out of your pre-tax or post-tax earnings. That's perfectly normal. You may not know whether you have or need life, disability, or liability insurance. You may have no idea how to prioritize cash savings, retirement savings, student loan repayments, saving for a house, or paying a mortgage. That's also perfectly normal.

I'm not going to tell you how to pick stocks, trade options, or get rich quick. I'm not going to assume that we know now what the concept of retirement, tax policy, or the general economy will look like four decades from now. I'm also not going to say that having a lot of money is essential—but I'm also not going to say that money doesn't matter, because that's simply not true.

What I *will* do is teach you the basics of building wealth: how to optimize your cash flows, how to reduce debt and learn to invest, how to pay less in taxes, and finally, how to protect your assets (once you have them) from many of the curveballs life might throw at you.

You're going to learn how to think about money in a way that will help you achieve future wealth and security. And you're going to learn how certain realities about living as young people today may have affected our collective mindset with regards to money and our idea of what it means to have quality of life—and how *that* ties in with our spending and financial behavior.

The next chapter is a foundational chapter with background

information you need in order to understand where we are and how we got here. Beginning in chapter 2, I'll help you create the framework for an organized, comprehensive, and personalized financial plan—just like the ones I create for my financial planning clients every day. You'll have to fill in your specific details, but I've given you the structure you'll need in order to do so. After that, we'll cover strategic cash flow planning, debt reduction, investing, tax planning, and asset protection. By the end of the book, you should have a clear and actionable plan for building wealth.

But you know what they say about people who don't learn from history being doomed to repeat it. Before we can look forward, we must take a look back, at the financial histories of our parents' generation through to our generation, to examine how we got to where we are now, and how it should inform our path forward.

CHAPTER 1

THE LANDSCAPE

Meet Amanda.

Amanda is thirty-three years old, a millennial. Her parents, Bob and Beth, are baby boomers. Amanda was raised in happy, upper-middle-class surroundings. Beth was a stay-at-home mom, and Bob got a bachelor's degree from a state university and spent most of his career working his way up the corporate ladder at a Fortune 500 company.

Bob and Beth bought a four-bedroom house in the suburbs of Chicago, and Bob commuted forty-five minutes each way to work each day. Bob's income allowed them to comfortably pay their mortgage, drive nice cars, and take regular family vacations. Beth had minimal need for childcare, due to working in the home. Bob will retire at age sixty-six with a fully paid-off home, $1 million saved into retirement accounts, and a pension of $1,200 per month, plus Social Security for the rest of his life. He'll likely spend twenty to thirty comfortable years in retirement.

There was never a question of whether Amanda would attend college—it was a given. Amanda's parents (and, thus, Amanda herself) saw a college degree as a sure path to financial success and opportunity, as it had been for Bob. Amanda's parents paid for her to attend a state university, where she earned a bachelor's degree in marketing.

She graduated from college in the midst of the economic recovery from the global financial crisis of 2008. Jobs were scarce, but after some months of applying, she was able to get a job doing digital marketing in Manhattan. In 2010, Amanda made $45,000 per year. She wasn't able to afford an apartment on her own, so she lived with a roommate and paid $1,700 per month for her half of a two-bedroom apartment. She had very little money left over to put into savings after paying for housing and other basic expenses each month, but it didn't worry her too much because most of her friends were in the same boat. She was young and living in one of the best cities in the world. Life was good—and she had plenty of time to start saving later.

After several years of working, it became clear that there was little room for income mobility in her chosen career track. In search of a brighter future, Amanda decided to attend business school, in hopes that an MBA would open new doors and launch her into a more lucrative career. She spent two years in business school full-time, accumulating $120,000 in student loan debt with an interest rate of 6 percent.

Shortly after graduating from business school, she married John, a man from her program. John had $250,000 in student loan debt from his undergraduate studies and business school, also at 6 percent interest. Amanda and John were both able to find jobs in Chicago after business school, after several months of applying. Together, they make $280,000 per year, though they are disappointed to find that they are now working in jobs that wouldn't have required an MBA just a few years ago.

After learning that they were expecting their first child, Amanda and John decided to pull the trigger on buying their first home. Three-bedroom homes near their workplaces average $700,000. Homes in the most desirable neighborhoods are in the millions. Amanda and John had $60,000 saved into a checking account for a down payment and small 401(k) accounts from former jobs. They purchased a modest three-bedroom house just outside the city for $600,000 and used $50,000 of their savings as an 8-percent down payment. This left them with a mortgage balance of $550,000 at 4 percent interest.

After the baby arrived, Amanda's job provided her with three months of unpaid maternity leave, after which she went back to work full-time *and* took on the new expense of childcare at $1,400 per month. They also financed a used SUV purchase in anticipation of the new baby—$5,000 down with $15,000 financed at 5 percent.

Between their student loans, mortgage, and car loan, Amanda and John now carry over $900,000 in debt. Childcare and debt payments take up a substantial portion of their monthly income. They have no idea when they will ever get to a zero net worth, let alone begin building wealth.

THE DIFFERENCE BETWEEN BOOMERS AND MILLENNIALS

As you may have guessed, Amanda is an avatar—a compilation of the stories that I hear every day from my clients, friends, and other millennials like you and me. She represents a common path taken by members of our generation, one that is vastly different than the path laid out before our baby boomer parents at the same age.

WHAT IS A BOOMER?

According to most definitions, baby boomers were born between 1946 and 1964. This is generally the generation in which our parents were born and came of age. The baby boomer generation graduated from college in the late seventies to early eighties, for the most part.

Adjusted for inflation, the cost of living was much lower for baby boomers entering adulthood than it was (and is) for millennials, especially with regard to housing and higher education. Millennials buying their first home today will pay on average 39 percent more than baby boomers did in the 1980s.[2] As most of us are keenly aware, the cost of getting a college education has also skyrocketed, with the annual cost of a four-year public university education growing more than *3,700 percent* between 1964 and 2015.[3]

To make matters worse, wages have not kept pace with the rapidly increasing costs of these basic adulthood milestones. Many baby boomers were able to obtain college and graduate degrees at a relatively low cost. Those degrees then launched them into stable, well-paying, long-term careers that allowed them to buy homes and start families.

Adding to the baby boomer generation's good fortune is the fact that they were starting their careers and families in and around the 1980s, the beginning of one of the great-

2 Shannon Insler, "Do Millennials Have It Better or Worse Than Generations Past?" StudentLoanHero.com, updated May 30, 2018, https://studentloanhero.com/featured/millennials-have-better-worse-than-generations-past/.

3 Joel Anderson, "Boomers vs. Millennials: A Look at the Financial Gap Between Generations," *Yahoo! Finance*, May 3, 2019, https://finance.yahoo.com/news/boomers-vs-millennials-look-financial-201000886.html.

est periods of economic growth in American history. They enjoyed almost two decades of low unemployment, high GDP and wage growth, amazing stock market returns, and boundless optimism.

WHAT IS A MILLENNIAL?

Millennials, on the other hand, were born between 1981 and 1996. Most millennials came of age around the Great Recession and were marked by the pervasive economic uncertainty of that time.

We faced some really tough macroeconomic trends: high unemployment, globalization, tuition inflation (and a growing reliance on student debt), changes in the need for skilled workers, stagnant wages, and vast increases in the costs of healthcare and housing. The world changed, and suddenly the sure path to success that worked for our parents seemed impossible for us to replicate.

There are currently about 75 million millennials in the US.[4] We are the largest generation, and we may be the first American generation to have a lower standard of living than our parents had. The idea that, through hard work, each generation builds a life for its children that is better than

4 Richard Fry, "Millennials Overtake Baby Boomers as America's Largest Generation," Pew Research Center, April 28, 2020, https://www.pewresearch.org/fact-tank/2020/04/28/millennials-overtake-baby-boomers-as-americas-largest-generation/.

they had for themselves has long been a part of the American dream. Whether millennials can overcome the unique obstacles they've faced to have better lives than the boomers remains to be seen.

A research and advocacy group called Young Invincibles, backed by the Ford Foundation, did a massive study on the financial health of millennials, measuring income, retirement savings, homeownership, assets, and net worth.[5] They found that millennials are the most educated, most diverse, and most indebted generation in American history.

Let's look at some of their key findings.

1. **Millennials earn less than their parents did.** Adjusted for inflation, millennials earn 20 percent less than our parents did at the same age. That means that we're potentially on track for lower lifetime earnings because incomes generated in the first decade of work often set the stage for lifetime earnings. Entering the workforce during an economic downturn meant that millennials had very few job options upon graduation. With little experience to offer, negotiating pay was not an option for most millennials in the difficult labor market that followed the Great Recession.

5 "Financial Health of Young America: Measuring Generational Declines between Baby Boomers and Millennials," Young Invincibles, January 2017, https://younginvincibles.org/wp-content/uploads/2017/04/FHYA-Final2017-1-1.pdf.

2. **Fewer millennials own homes.** Home ownership has long been a larger part of the American dream. Particularly for people in the middle class, building equity in a home over decades is a major way to realize a positive net worth. Millennials, though, are much less likely to own their home than Boomers were at the same age.
3. **Millennials have accumulated half the assets of boomers.** The study specifically says that, "When baby boomers were young adults, they owned twice the assets of young adults in 2013." (It isn't surprising that we own less considering that we're earning less!)
4. **We have more student loan debt.** The millennial student loan debt burden is close to $500 billion.[6] And student loans are generally saddled with relatively high interest rates, so they can turn into what I call "compounding monsters" if not addressed wisely. This, combined with low asset ownership and low wages, is a recipe for financial hardship.

BUT IT'S NOT ALL SUNSHINE AND ROSES FOR BOOMERS

As I write this in 2020, we are watching what many are calling a baby boomer retirement crisis start to unfold.

Baby boomers are retiring at a rate of around 10,000 people a

6 Wesley Whistle, "A Look at Millennial Student Debt," *Forbes*, October 3, 2019, https://www.forbes.com/sites/wesleywhistle/2019/10/03/a-look-at-millennial-student-debt/#7f9a5a4f2437.

day. Nearly half of them were already retired as of 2019. Also in 2019, as reported by the Insured Retirement Institute, "45 percent of baby boomers have *no* retirement savings."[7] That's right—none. Hard to believe, right? Thus, approximately half of retirees are or will be living entirely off Social Security benefits—a scary thought, especially when you consider that one partner will survive until at least the age of ninety-five in almost half of sixty-five-year-old married couples.[8]

The study surveyed retirees and found that that their top two regrets for life involved bad financial planning: 63 percent wish they had saved more, and 58 percent wish they had started saving earlier.

> One of the factors in these regrets—and one that could have made a massive difference in their outcomes—is their financial behavior (which is the topic of chapter 2).

So, baby boomers aren't doing so well after all, and they certainly shouldn't be envied by us. Even Bob the Baby Boomer (described earlier in this chapter), who retired with $1 million, Social Security, and a pension, isn't in the *best* position. As we'll discuss in chapter 3, lump sums of savings don't stretch nearly as far most people assume, and it's

7 Boomer Expectations for Retirement 2019," Insured Retirement Institute, April 2019, https://www.myirionline.org/docs/default-source/default-document-library/iri_babyboomers_whitepaper_2019_final.pdf?sfvrsn=0&mod=article_inline.

8 Ibid.

likely that Bob and Beth will have to tighten their belts in retirement to avoid running out of money.

You may be surprised to hear this, but things are looking pretty good for us relative to the boomers. As Warren Buffett says, "It's good to learn from your mistakes. It's better to learn from other people's mistakes." If we can learn from their mistakes and make better choices going forward, we have a good shot of ending up in a good place. And we have at our disposal one very important resource that they have much less of: time.

But how did an entire generation blessed with so many economic advantages screw up in such a colossal way?

EXPENSIVE MISTAKES

We've already acknowledged that we're starting from behind. A lot of us are just trying to get to a zero net worth, which would be a great victory because getting to zero is the first step to building a positive net worth.

Much of the millennials-versus-boomers narrative focuses on how the boomers were at a zero net worth (or higher) straight out of school. But does that really matter now?

Despite the economic abundance that boomers enjoyed early on, they made a lot of mistakes. They *way* under saved and took on too much debt, severely underestimating how much they spent and overestimating how far their savings would go. They placed enormous faith in the government and outside institutions to provide for their later years through pensions and Social Security—and this turned out to be a risky bet. If you watch the headlines, you'll see that many pension funds are in big trouble, unable to pay the benefits they promised boomers decades ago (ironically due to poor planning, which is also why boomers are in the position to depend on pensions in the first place). Some pensions are even straight-up going bust. The future of Social Security is also quite uncertain, with many projections putting it as likely to run out of money within the next fifteen years unless cuts are made.[9] This is a scenario that many baby boomers did not plan for.

It's unlikely that our generation will have pensions or Social Security at our disposal as we reach retirement age (if we are even able to "retire" in the sense that older generations do now). If we do, great! But one thing that has become very clear is that the only people we can *truly* rely on for our own future financial security are ourselves—and there is great power in that realization.

We have a lot of positives on our side, too, like time and knowledge. We have so many technological tools that weren't

9 Stephen C. Goss, "The Future Financial Status of the Social Security Program," *Social Security Bulletin* 70, no. 3 (2010): https://www.ssa.gov/policy/docs/ssb/v70n3/v70n3p111.html.

available to previous generations—learning about and tracking your finances has never been easier. If we leverage the abundance of resources we have to take control of our financial futures now, we *can* build wealth and financial security, possibly even more than previous generations.

IT'S NOT FAIR

A big part of the millennial financial shtick is how cruel life has been to our generation. We got dealt a bad hand. It's not *fair*.

And as a millennial, I tend to agree. But so what? Where is that mindset getting us? If we want to end up in a better place than the baby boomers, we need to stop dwelling on the unfairness of it all and shift focus to building a better future for ourselves.

Here's one of my biggest takeaways from my work as a financial planner: for most people, *behavior* is the number-one factor that differentiates those who build wealth from those who do not. And that's a good thing because behavior, unlike economic conditions, is within your control. In the next chapter, we'll explore the topic of financial behavior and discuss how you can use positive financial behaviors to better your life and build wealth.

LET'S BREAK IT DOWN

- Millennials have faced unique obstacles to building wealth, including: periods of high unemployment, globalization, tuition inflation (and a growing reliance on student debt), changes in the need for skilled workers, stagnant wages, and vast increases in the costs of healthcare and housing.
- We earn less income, have less assets, and have more debt than our parents' generation did at our age.
- However, our parents' generation is facing an unprecedented retirement crisis due to poor planning and bad financial behavior.
- We have two invaluable resources on our side: time and the ability to learn from the mistakes of those who came before us. If we use these resources wisely, we *can* overcome the unique obstacles we face to build wealth.

CHAPTER 2

FINANCIAL BEHAVIOR

James and Lauren are family friends of mine. They met in Madagascar, where they were both serving in the Peace Corps, and eloped in Southeast Asia after their Peace Corps work ended. Today, they both work in the nonprofit world and are the quintessential optimistic do-gooders. They're certainly not in it for the money—together, they make around $100,000 per year.

In Washington, DC, where the cost of living is quite high, $100,000 doesn't go very far. But James and Lauren are very frugal by nature, their time in the Peace Corps enlightening them as to what's a *need* versus a *want*. Because of this, they manage to live quite well—*and* within their means.

In fact, James and Lauren are well on their way to financial independence and are in a better financial position than many people I know who make many times their income.

I realized this when James was laid off from his job during the global pandemic. I was worried for them, having assumed that they lived on a shoestring. I offered to do some free financial planning for them, thinking that they would certainly welcome some advice on how to make ends meet.

As it turned out, they had:

- A rainy day fund with eight months of expenses in cash.
- Roth IRAs, which they fully funded each year.
- *Very* low living expenses, which makes sense, given that they were able to live *and* save while making relatively little for the DC area.

All things considered, they were fine! James was confident that he would gain new employment within a few months, and they could easily pay expenses with savings in the meantime. I was shocked and just had to ask, "How did you manage this?"

"Well, it's actually pretty simple," Lauren said. "We were only making around $70,000 together when we started out working on the Hill after leaving the Peace Corps. We've had pretty steady increases in pay since then, but we haven't changed our lifestyle much. We started saving a good portion of each increase in income. We probably live as if we only made around $80,000, which now allows us to save almost a quarter of our income."

They remind me of Jim and Margie, extended family members of mine who are now in their eighties. As retired school teachers, they've always lived modestly. But they were also frugal by nature and lived well within their means for most of their lives. They retired with a paid-off home and a nest egg that would allow them to live the lifestyle to which they'd become accustomed for the remainder of their lives.

Several years ago, they inherited a little over $1 million from a relative. So, what did they do—upgrade their home, travel, go on a spending spree? Nope. They called my firm to ask for help: "We have no idea what to do with this money. We don't need it!"

Ultimately, they decided to invest it for the long-term, with the intent that their children will inherit a nice investment portfolio someday. It's been years, and they've never touched a dime.

OH, BEHAVE

When it comes to financial behavior, James and Lauren are not the norm—even I have trouble relating to their thrifty lifestyle.

Like most things, financial behavior exists on a spectrum. James, Lauren, Jim, and Margie are towards the frugal end of the spectrum. On the other end of the spectrum are people who spend everything they earn *and more*, whether they're making $80,000 or $800,000 a year. This spectrum is the reason we generally shouldn't conflate *wealth* with *income*. Having wealth means having a high net worth. Many people assume that high earners must be wealthy, when that is often far from the truth.

I know a couple—let's call them Matt and Shannon—that makes roughly $800,000 per year together, but they are far from wealthy—and in danger of never reaching financial independence. Despite making eight times what James and Lauren make, they can't seem to save more than $40,000 a year. Beyond that, they spend just about everything that's left after taxes.

How can a couple that's used to spending close to half a million dollars each year accumulate enough savings to maintain that lifestyle if they're only saving $40,000 a year? I've run the numbers, and they don't add up. Sadly, this couple will be chained to their incomes—and, thus, their jobs—unless they decide to make a dramatic lifestyle change.

If either of them had been laid off, as James had, during the COVID-19 pandemic, they would have been in a bad place, and possibly unable to pay regular expenses after a short amount of time. They are high earners, and they may have more assets than James and Lauren, but they are much further from financial independence.

> Growing up, I always adored my friend Julie's mom. She was an attorney with a seemingly high-powered and glamorous career. She was impeccably dressed, drove a gorgeous Porsche, and lived in a well-appointed penthouse condo on the water. She was *rich*—or so I assumed.
>
> Flash forward a decade later, as I caught up with Julie over drinks and she shared some unfortunate news: her mom was borderline broke.
>
> Julie had approached her mom for financial help with her grad school tuition, only to have her mom tell her that she "just can't swing it."
>
> "How can that be?" Julie asked.
>
> Well, as it turned out, the Porsche was leased for $1,300 a month. Julie's mom had recently taken a second mortgage on her condo to pay off a bunch of credit card debt she'd accumulated shopping, only to accumulate more credit card debt. She was leveraged to the hilt, barely able to cover her debt payments and other monthly expenses. If she lost her job, she'd have to give up the Porsche and the penthouse. Approaching sixty, she was severely under-saved for retirement and would either have to work for decades more or make dramatic lifestyle cuts. She felt like a hamster on a wheel.
>
> I was beyond shocked to hear that my childhood hero was all smoke and mirrors—but it was a great lesson. For the first time, I considered that outward signals of wealth don't guarantee that actual wealth exists behind the curtain. In fact, outward signals of wealth might ironically be the very cause of financial instability, as in this case.

The takeaway here is that income and wealth are not the same thing. To be even more specific, high income does not necessarily lead to wealth or financial independence.

So what accounts for these scenarios where people with lower incomes are able to achieve financial independence while people with higher incomes do not?

Behavior.

MILLIONAIRES NEXT DOOR

Lauren and James are great examples of the "millionaires next door," a term coined by Thomas J. Stanley and William D. Danko's bestselling book, *The Millionaire Next Door*.

In the course of researching their book, Stanley and Danko were surprised to find more millionaires living in blue-collar neighborhoods than in white-collar neighborhoods. As it turned out, people living in white-collar neighborhoods were more likely to spend their incomes on luxury items and wealth signifiers than to use their higher incomes to accumulate true wealth.

The authors went on to characterize people as Under Accumulators of Wealth (UAWs) or Prodigious Accumulators of Wealth (PAWs). UAWs are people who have a low net worth relative to their income, whereas PAWs are the opposite—

people who have a high net worth relative to their income. What made someone a PAW versus a UAW? Again: *behavior*.

Matt and Shannon are classic UAWs. They make a lot, and they spend a lot. Their net worth is very low relative to their income, and it's not growing nearly enough for them to reach financial independence anytime soon. James and Lauren, on the other hand, are prototypical PAWs. Although they are not high earners, they are rapidly accumulating assets. Their net worth is high relative to their incomes, and it is trending upward. If they stay on track, they will eventually become millionaires next door.

F-YOU MONEY

My parents have always lived within their means. They did well, but they also didn't spend a lot. The cost of living is quite low where I grew up, so they were able to save close to 50 percent of their joint income in the early years of their careers. This frugality, combined with prudent investing, paid off big. Once they hit mid-life, they realized that their wealth had grown to the point where they could pretty much do whatever they wanted for the rest of their lives, within reason. They had total financial independence. They had F-you money.

I learned the true meaning of financial independence in my late twenties when I got into a snowmobile accident and racked up some massive medical bills. The bill for my air ambulance alone was $55,000. My health insurer paid $7,000 and called it a day, leaving me to deal with the balance. Before long, I had debt collectors from the air ambulance company calling me on a regular basis. It was an incredibly stressful time for me. There were some days when I felt like dealing with financial fallout was more painful than the actual accident.

Up until this point, I'd felt like I was on a great financial path. I was a professional, *responsible* financial planner with zero debt. I had accumulated a nest egg that I was quite proud of between my 401k and savings. And I lived within my means, never worrying about money.

Despite all of this, I was not in a position to pay nearly $70,000 in total out-of-pocket medical and dental costs. I debated not paying the air ambulance anything more. I wanted to tell them to take their $7,000 and F off—but I knew that I would regret that for the rest of my life. You see, as a young person just starting out in the world, I needed good credit, and telling the air ambulance jerks to F off would likely tank my credit score. I felt powerless, like my hard-earned nest egg was no longer my own.

Contrast my experience with medical bills with my dad's. My dad is a physician and the type of guy who's always looking for a deal. In advance of a routine medical procedure, he called his doctor's office and asked if there was a lower "cash price" if he didn't bill it through insurance. Sure enough, there was. He arranged to pay the cash price and went ahead with the procedure. Several weeks later, a bill arrived in the mail that was nearly three times what he had agreed to pay. Something had been lost in translation. After arguing with the physician and his insurer to no avail, he mailed the physician a check for the amount he had agreed to pay. For him, it wasn't about the money—it was about the principle.

A long back and forth ensued, and the physician's office let my dad know that they were sending him to collections for his unpaid balance. "That's fine," my dad said to the medical billing administrator who had been calling regularly.

"This will ruin your credit," she warned.

"Go ahead, I don't need credit," Dad said, as he hung up.

Unlike me, he was totally free, beholden to no one.

We should all aim to achieve this kind of financial independence—the kind where you owe the world nothing, and your most precious resources, such as time and money, are truly your own. In more concrete terms, this means having a net worth that is large enough to sustain your chosen lifestyle for the rest of your life, without being dependent on any other source for income or credit.

So what does this mean for you?

Maybe it means that you don't have to work a traditional job anymore, and that you can explore doing what's meaningful to you. Both of my parents abruptly switched careers once they reached the point of true financial independence and are now pursuing their passions—art and financial planning. Maybe it means taking less crap and being able to say F you a little more.

What it takes to achieve this level of financial freedom will vary from person to person. If you live in an area with a low cost of living, then the net worth you'll need to accumulate to be financially independent will be lower than what's needed for someone living in an expensive area. If you can find a geographic arbitrage—earning a lot of money while living in a low-cost area, as my parents did—it will be even easier.

Of course, whether or not your chosen lifestyle involves spending a lot of money is a big factor, too. Quality of life is all about perspective. As Chris Rock says, "If Bill Gates woke up with Oprah's money, he'd jump out the window."

CHANGE YOUR FINANCIAL BEHAVIOR

As it turns out, we (as humans, not just millennials) don't always act rationally, despite the claims of traditional economic theory, which posits that we are rational actors. In reality, we often behave in a way that runs contrary to our own best interests—financially and otherwise.

That's why behavioral finance, a relatively new field of study, has become increasingly important in academia. In fact, six Nobel prizes have been awarded for behavioral finance research.

And, as you've probably gathered by now, the takeaway from this chapter is that behavior is often the biggest factor affecting financial outcomes, good and bad.

People who build wealth tend to earn a decent income, live within their means, avoid excessive debt, and invest in a wise, disciplined manner. They also tend to avoid lifestyle creep, which we'll discuss in the next chapter. People who end up without wealth later in life tend to spend more than they make, finance their spending with excessive debt, and invest foolishly, if at all.

Good financial behavior leads to having options, flexibility, and autonomy. The consequences of bad financial behavior, on the other hand, include a lack of options and lack of control over how you spend your time and money.

Knowing that behavior is the biggest differentiator in building wealth is a *good* thing, because your behavior is something that is totally within your control. We can't control the state of the economy, stock market movements, or whether a global pandemic causes millions of people to become ill and lose their jobs all at the same time. But we can, through positive behavior, become financially bulletproof, prepared to weather any storm.

And don't worry if you don't yet know where you're starting from or how to get where you're going—I have a five-step plan I call your Personal Financial Audit to get you on the right path.

STEP ONE: CONFRONT YOUR FINANCIAL REALITY

The first step to getting on the path to financial independence is confronting your financial reality. A high net worth should be your end goal, so ascertaining your current net worth should be your jumping-off point.

When I first sit down with a new client, I ask:

- How much do you have?
- How much do you owe?
- How much do you make?
- How much do you spend?
- How much do you save?

These high-level questions may sound simple, but most people can't give full answers to all of these questions without doing some digging.

Figuring out your net worth is as simple as answering the first two questions: how much you have and how much you owe. Subtract how much you owe from how much you have, and that's your net worth.

For example, John has:

- Roughly $120,000 in home equity (which is what you could sell your home for minus your mortgage balance)
- $85,000 in retirement accounts
- $15,000 in cash on hand

John owes:

- $8,000 in auto debt
- $5,000 on credit cards yet to be paid off
- $40,000 in student loan debt

John's net worth = ($120,000 + $85,000 + $15,000)—($8,000 + $5,000 + $40,000)= $167,000

You don't need to get too granular here. You certainly don't need to include the value of every personal item you own—and you shouldn't, because most personal possessions depreciate in value (vehicles and most jewelry are great examples) and are "use" assets that would not count as part of a nest egg that you can draw from in the future.

How you run this calculation is up to you. You can go old school with pen and paper, you can throw it into Excel, or you can you use an online calculator (my preferred method). NerdWallet and Bankrate have great online net worth calculators.

After you find your net worth, you will want to get a big picture idea of your cash flow situation—in other words, where is your money going? You can figure this out by answering the bottom three questions: what you make, what you spend, what you save.

Figuring out what you make is the easiest part of this step for most people. If you're salaried, just pull a pay stub.* If your pay is more complex, because you're self-employed or your pay is dependent on commissions or bonuses, you may have to make some projections (but err on the conservative side). Pulling your prior year tax return is usually helpful.

*Note: Pulling a paystub is a great way to learn a lot about your gross income versus net income and what specifically is taken out of your paycheck (income taxes, payroll taxes, benefits withholding, retirement funding, etc.).

For example, Sarah, who is a salaried employee paid bi-monthly, pulled her most recent paystub, dated 6/30/2020. It shows that she has been paid close to $70,000 year-to-date. She can deduce that she is on track to make around $140,000 for the year. It also shows that around $17,000 has been withheld from her pay year-to-date for state income tax, federal income tax, and payroll taxes. Her net (after-tax) pay per pay period is $3,420. So she knows that she's got $6,840 hitting her bank account each month.

Once you know what you make, you need to figure out where it's all going. For starters, do you actively set aside savings? If so, how much, how often, and where does it go? If not, do you have money left over at the end of each month? Getting a comprehensive picture of what you make versus what you spend can be tricky. I recommend pulling a year of statements for every credit card, bank account, and any other account where money goes in or out, so you can track the flow of money for each.

Sarah, from the above example, pulled monthly statements for all bank and credit accounts for 2020, year-to date. What she found surprised her:

- $6,840 hit her bank account each month.
- Of that, $3,000 went to fixed expenses like housing costs and bills.
- $500 each month went to a separate savings account.
- Nearly all other expenses were paid on a combination of credit cards, with an average total credit card bill of $4,200 each month.

That didn't add up! She made $6,840, saved $500, and spent $7,700? How is that possible?

Well, her growing credit card balance might explain it. As it turns out, the $500 per month savings had been giving her a false sense of security. Sarah's spending is causing her net worth to move in the wrong direction.

Of course, the inputs and outputs to these net worth and cash flow questions will vary from person to person.

And I'll be honest—this part sucks for a lot of people. If looking at your cash flows or debts is something you've been avoiding, it's probably because you're scared of what you'll find. But sticking your head in the sand is not the answer. The feeling of temporary comfort it may provide is not worth the long-term financial consequences. My advice is to rip off the Band-Aid. Do this work and gain an understanding of where you're at now, so you can get started on taking control of your future.

STEP TWO: EDUCATE YOURSELF

Now that you have an understanding of your net worth and cash flows, you need some context within which to view them. This means gaining a baseline understanding of personal finance. Your chances of success are relatively low if you approach this totally blind; it's hard to make good financial decisions if you're operating in a vacuum without any understanding of debt, investing, taxes, or asset protection.

The good news is that you don't have to go very far to get started on that. I wrote this book with the intention that it would be a one-stop-shop for the average millennial trying to gain a basic knowledge of personal finance. I tried to make this well rounded and comprehensive but with no more detail than the average person needs to know on any given topic.

There's no shortage of resources if you're looking to take a deeper dive into any of the subjects I address in this book, as a quick Google search will show you, and I encourage you to go deeper if you have the interest.

STEP THREE: SET GOALS

So, what good is all this new financial knowledge if you're not channeling it towards bettering your future? Goal setting is an essential part of any good financial plan. Having concrete financial goals will give you focus, direction, and accountability as you get on the path to building wealth.

Much of the financial advice given to the baby boomer generation was fixated on achieving retirement. Now, we can see that retirement in and of itself is not a helpful goal because we're all going to retire (in some form) regardless. But *we* want to retire in a place of comfort, stability, and security—in other words, with positive outcomes—and that means financial independence, rather than retirement, should be your ultimate goal.

By financial independence, I mean a net worth large enough to sustain your desired lifestyle for the rest of your life, regardless of your future access to income or credit.

As the FIRE movement (discussed in the Introduction) shows, it is possible to achieve long-term financial independence with a relatively low net worth if you're willing to live *very* modestly. If that's for you, great. If you're a little more high maintenance (like me), you'll need to accumulate more.

There will be many more immediate, micro-level goals that you'll need to set as necessary prerequisites to amassing a net worth large enough to make you financially independent. How much you should accumulate, and the incremental steps you'll need to take to get there, will vary from person to person. In chapter 3, I'll help you nail down what your specific goals should be—but many of us should be shooting to accumulate millions. More on that later.

STEP FOUR: MAKE A PLAN TO ACHIEVE YOUR GOALS

Of course, the next step in your Personal Financial Audit exercise is making a plan to achieve your goal.

Chapters 3 through 7 of this book will help with that, too. A well-rounded financial plan for the average millennial trying to build wealth should cover:

- Cash-flow planning to build wealth (chapter 3).
- Debt reduction (chapter 4).
- Investing (chapter 5).
- Tax planning (chapter 6).
- Building your own safety net through insurance and asset protection (chapter 7).

If you read and follow the advice in the rest of this book, you should be able to write out a personalized, actionable financial plan specific to your goals and circumstances. If your situation is complex, or if you need additional help, you always have the option of engaging a professional financial planner.

> If it's your first time looking for or talking to a financial planner, beware that unfortunately the financial advice industry is loaded with people trying to make a buck by selling you things you don't need. Make sure that you hire someone who is:
>
> - A Certified Financial Planner™. You can find one near you by visiting the CFP Board's website, www.letsmakeaplan.org.
> - Fee-only. This means that they are paid by you and you alone. They do not earn commissions or kickbacks from selling you financial products.
> - A fiduciary to you, meaning that they have taken an oath to put their clients' interests before their own at all times.

I do realize, however, that not everybody is in the position to be able to hire a financial planner—and that was a big consideration for me in writing this book.

STEP FIVE: CONTINUALLY TRACK AND EVALUATE WHERE YOU ARE RELATIVE TO YOUR GOALS

Finally, step five to getting on the path to financial independence is continually tracking and evaluating where you are relative to your goals.

My experience has been that people tend to have an impetus for goal setting—a freak-out over their future, for example, or a distressing setback—which leads to an energetic session of thinking and planning. Too often, however, that energy and motivation trickles away leaving all those well-intentioned plans dead in the water.

This is human nature—for all sorts of planning and goal-setting—but it's a behavior you can change.

When it comes to building wealth, it's essential to continually track where you are and what direction you're heading in. How are you going to achieve your goals if you don't know how close you are or if you've gotten off track?

Your financial plan shouldn't be a static snapshot of your life frozen at one point in time. A good financial plan should evolve and keep up with your life. Our lives change all the time. If you look at where you were five years ago, it probably doesn't look exactly like where you are today—or where you'd like to be in another five years. This is especially true from a financial perspective, and even more so at our phase in life, when we are increasing our earnings, possibly going back to school, buying our first homes, and starting families. This is a dynamic time.

While your global macro goal of amassing a high net worth probably won't change, the specifics of your path there will likely need to be recalibrated from time to time. That doesn't mean that you have to start from scratch every month, but you should do a thorough review of your progress and plan as a whole at least once per year, with monthly or quarterly tracking and status updates in the meantime. This shouldn't be one of those New Year's resolutions that starts strong on January first but dies out by the tenth.

Your annual review should cover: your net worth, cash flows, debts, investments, taxes, and financial safety net.

In the following chapters, I'll elaborate on the specifics of how to review each of these topics annually as part of your financial plan review and which parts you should consider tracking more frequently.

FROM HERE TO THERE

One of my favorite clients is Tim, a physician and recent immigrant in his mid-thirties who was the first person in his family to go to college. I first met Tim when he was fresh out of residency and had six figures of student loan debt from medical school. He'd been referred by another physician in his practice and he needed a financial plan, as he was high on debts and low on assets.

I wrote up a financial plan that primarily focused on paying off his loans and sent him on his way, expecting that it would be at least four or five years before his student loans were paid down. Eighteen months later, he was debt-free and questioning what to do with all of the extra cash he was accumulating now that his loans were done. He'd made around $60,000 a year as a resident. He was now making around $320,000 per year, but his lifestyle and spending had barely changed. He was still, as they say, "living like a resident," on roughly 20 percent of his income.

This short-term choice had tremendous payoff. Two years into practice, he was debt-free and on track to become quite wealthy within a matter of time. His biggest problem was figuring out what to do with all of his extra cash now that the loans were paid off—and learning how to spend a little more money on himself.

We updated his financial plan with a focus on making incremental increases to his quality of life, while also saving and investing aggressively so he would have the option of retiring in his fifties, which was his primary goal. Since then, Tim has bought a house and a very fun car, and is helping his nephews pay for college. He's continued to increase his income and is rapidly accumulating wealth.

Now, you may be thinking, "Sure, it's *easy* to build wealth on a physician's income."

I can tell you from experience that it's not easy for almost *anyone* to live on a lot less than they make. It actually requires a lot of discipline and commitment. I've worked with plenty of other physicians who also made $60,000 per year as residents, and then promptly began spending 90 percent of their newly high incomes early in practice.

Tim's story is inspirational to me, and it reminds me of a great point from Dr. Meg Jay's book, *The Defining Decade: Why Your Twenties Matter and How to Make the Most of Them Now*. People in their twenties, she says, "...are like airplanes, just taking off from LAX heading for somewhere west. A slight change in course on takeoff is the difference between ending up in Alaska or Fiji."

A huge part of Tim's future financial success will be due to these choices he made early in his career. Becoming debt-free so early in life will have a massive impact on his ability to build wealth.

And this applies for you, too. It doesn't matter where you are now. Maybe you're nothing like Tim—maybe you're making bupkis and you're in debt up to your ears. Maybe you have a spending problem. But you're relatively young, and you're reading this book, which means you probably want to take your future into your own hands. And the good news is, it's not too late. When it comes to building wealth, time is the most precious resource. And you are *rich* with time.

If you're in your twenties or thirties, you're just like that plane taking off from LAX. If you start now, making even incremental steps in the right direction can have an outsized impact on your destination. But the longer you wait, the more difficult it will be to change course. So don't wait. Let's not end up like the baby boomers—out of time and out of money, after decades of kicking the can down the road.

If you're ready to roll up your sleeves and get to work, then chapter 3, on cash flow planning, is waiting for you.

LET'S BREAK IT DOWN

- High income and high wealth (and low income and low wealth) do not necessarily go hand-in-hand.
- Behavior is the biggest differentiator between those who build wealth and those who do not. This is a good thing, because it's fully within your control.
- Your goal should be to accumulate a net worth large enough to grant you financial independence: the ability to live your desired lifestyle without relying on anyone else for income or credit.

You can get on the path to financial independence by changing your financial behavior, and you can start by conducting a five-step Personal Financial Audit:

1. Confront your financial reality.
2. Educate yourself.
3. Set goals.
4. Make a plan to achieve your goals.
5. Continually track and evaluate where you are relative to your goals.

CHAPTER 3

CASH FLOW PLANNING

So, how much do *you* need to save to achieve financial independence? I may have dropped a bit of a bomb on you at the end of the last chapter when I hinted that the magic number is likely in the millions. In this chapter, we'll get into why that is, and how you can use cash flow planning to get there.

Coming up with this magic number to shoot for is one of the first things I address with new clients. Many clients initially engage financial planners to address more immediate short-term concerns, such as student loan reduction or allocating an investment portfolio. But if you zoom out and take a 30,000-foot view, those concerns are all smaller prerequisite steps along the way to building a high net worth, which should be the big-picture goal.

Take Emma, for example. Emma initially engaged me in 2014 because she'd never so much as thought about a financial plan, and she wanted a professional to tell her that she was "okay financially." Here are my initial notes on Emma and the information I gathered after working with her to complete step 1 (Confronting Your Financial Reality) of the Personal Financial Audit exercise from chapter 2:

- Thirty-seven years old, consultant in Denver, CO.
- Single, no children, avid skier.
- Income around $250,000 per year (about $160,000 after taxes).
- Fixed expenses, including housing costs, totaled around $50,000 per year.
- Total assets: $520,000:
  - Equity in Condo: $170,000 (Fair Market Value of $420,000—Mortgage Balance of $250,000).
  - $350,000 in cash and retirement accounts.
- Additional debts: $20,000 auto loan at 5.2 percent.
- Net worth: $500,000.

We deduced that she was spending around $150,000 per year (around 93 percent of her post-tax income)—so she probably was not "okay" financially. Relative to her income, her fixed expenses were fairly low. Outside of making mortgage and car payments, she didn't have many other necessary expenses. I asked her if she knew where the rest of the money was going. "I don't live an extravagant life," she said. "It's hard for me to believe that I'm spending $90,000 a year on discretionary things."

After pulling a couple years of bank and credit card statements, we had a good idea of where the rest was going. About half of her discretionary spending went towards skiing, traveling, and dining out. The rest went to a mixture of things that I would consider to be "normal life stuff"—personal maintenance, gym memberships, dog walkers, groceries, Amazon purchases, shopping, etc.

Her cash flows and net worth gave us a good snapshot of where she was financially, but this information didn't mean much if we couldn't view it relative to where she wanted to end up. That's why the next step in developing a financial plan is goal setting, which allows you to view where you are within the context of where you'd like to go.

I like to begin the goal-setting process by asking clients the Three Kinder Questions, a set of questions developed by George Kinder, the founder of the Kinder Institute of Life Planning and author of *The Seven Stages of Money Maturity*. These questions are a great way to suss out what people want out of life and what truly matters to them. Once you know that, goal setting is easy. The three questions are:

1. Imagine you have enough money to satisfy all of your needs, now and in the future. Would you change your life and, if so, how would you change it?
2. This time, assume you are in your current financial situation. Your doctor tells you that you only have five to ten years to live, but that you will feel fine up until the end. Would you change your life and, if so, how would you change it?
3. Your doctor tells you that you have just one day to live. You look back at your life. What did you miss out on? Who did you not get to be? What did you fail to do?

Emma's answers to these questions made it very clear that her priorities were:

1. Working less
2. Skiing more

After more back and forth, we were able to whittle Emma's big-picture goal down to this: *Accumulate enough money to have financial independence* by age fifty-five, so she can ski at least 100 days per year from that point on.* This was the qualitative side of her goal.

*Notice that "retirement" is not mentioned at all here. As I mentioned in chapter 2, I think that focusing on retirement as a goal is missing the point, and doing this is one reason why baby boomers are facing a generational financial crisis. Many of them achieved their goal of retiring, meaning that they stopped working, but they're in danger of going broke. What good is that? Furthermore, we have no idea how the world will have changed decades from now, or what that could mean for work and the concept of "retirement." Retiring, in and of itself, does not mean that you're financially stable and does not guarantee happiness. Financial independence, on the other hand, certainly means the former and is more likely to lead to the latter.

Now we had to figure out the quantitative side of things.

We had two quantitative questions to answer: 1) what will her desired lifestyle cost annually? And 2) how much will she need to accumulate to live that lifestyle while maintaining financial independence, i.e., without reliance on outside sources for income or credit, by a given age?

Regarding the first question, Emma thought that she could have good quality of life for a lot less than she was currently spending each year—especially now that she realized that much of her discretionary spending was not in alignment with the things that truly mattered to her. "If I spent less on all this miscellaneous stuff, I could ski 100 days each year and *still* spend less than I do now," she said. Great! We projected that if she cut discretionary spending, she could live her desired lifestyle for a total cost of around

$90,000 per year. Obviously, this was a dramatic lifestyle cost reduction.

Onto the second question: How much would she need to accumulate to live her desired lifestyle by age fifty-five without relying on outside sources for income or credit going forward?

"Alright," I said, "if you want to spend around $90,000 per year starting in your fifties without having to depend on outside sources for income or credit, you should aim to accumulate *at least* $2.25 million in *liquid* assets by then."

She looked at me like I was insane.

NEVER UNDERESTIMATE

Like Emma, most people don't have a solid understanding of how far a given lump sum of savings will stretch. Remember the study by the Insured Retirement Institute that I mentioned in chapter 1? It found that 63 percent of baby boomers severely underestimated how far their savings would go in retirement.

And that's very easy to do because the math of how long a lump sum of money can provide income is actually pretty astounding. Using the 4 percent rule is my favorite way to illustrate this math.

The 4 percent rule is a financial planning rule of thumb typically used for determining the maximum amount of money a retiree can spend from a lump sum of savings each year without risking running out of money before death.

The original concept of the 4 percent rule is the result of a well-known study performed by a financial advisor named William Bengen in the 1990s. Bengen ran a bunch of models using the previous fifty years of historical data on stock and bond returns, which showed that taking withdrawals of *4 percent per year* from a lump sum *investment* portfolio was a sustainable rate of withdrawal with very little risk of depleting the lump sum over a *thirty-year period**—even during severe market downturns.

*Why thirty years? Because in the 1990s, most people retired in their sixties and could be expected to live for maybe another thirty years. This is useful for us as well, as we can extrapolate results for our estimated life expectancies.

This is also sometimes called the Safe Withdrawal Rule, because the sustainable withdrawal rate from a given lump sum is not always 4 percent. It may be higher or lower, depending on a variety of factors such as life expectancy. While 4 percent is the safe withdrawal rate over a thirty-year period, 5 percent to 6 percent would be considered sustainable over a twenty-year period. And longer withdrawal periods mean that the safe withdrawal rate should be lower than 4 percent.

Now, before we go any further, I do want to say that this is one of those topics that people in personal finance argue about all the time. If you do a quick online search along the lines of "Why the 4 percent rule is wrong," you'll find many articles pointing out exceptions, loopholes, and caveats to the 4 percent rule*—and most of these articles make great points. But that doesn't matter for our purposes here. We aren't using the 4 percent rule in its usual capacity—we aren't retirees trying to figure out how to not run out of money before we die. We're young accumulators trying to *estimate* what *minimum* net worth we should aim for to live with total financial independence. If we do this right, and invest well, the hope (and likelihood) is that we accumulate more than our minimum goal.**

*A common criticism of the 4 percent rule is that it's too conservative, and that strictly following this rule causes retirees to spend less than they "could"—leaving money on the table. While that may be true, I think that financial planning guidelines *should* err on the side of being conservative. As we face the baby boomer retirement crisis, I think we can all agree that many people of that generation would have been better off being more conservative with spending and retirement projections.

**This rule assumes that the lump sum is invested in a balanced portfolio of stocks and bonds (something I'll discuss more in chapter 5).

Here's how I used the 4 percent rule to come up with the $2.25 million liquid* net worth target for Emma:

- Emma wants to achieve a net worth large enough to sustain a $90,000 per year lifestyle with total financial independence by age fifty-five.
- Using the 4 percent rule as a guideline, I know that she would need roughly $1 million to sustain withdrawals of $40,000 per year over a thirty-year period without a high risk of running out of money.
- Per the Social Security Administration's Actuarial Life Expectancy tables, a fifty-five-year-old woman in the US is expected to live another 28.81 years.[10]
- This life expectancy of just under thirty years puts Emma's safe withdrawal rate right around 4 percent, per the Safe Withdrawal Rule.
- $90,000 is a 4 percent withdrawal of a $2.25 million lump sum.

*Liquid net worth refers to cash and liquid investments—not illiquid wealth, such as the equity you have in real estate, a closely-held business, etc. Think of it as money you could access for spending tomorrow if you needed to.

It's likely Emma will hit that goal if she starts saving now. I plugged her $2.25 million goal and her eighteen-year savings time period (the eighteen years she has from her current age, thirty-seven, until she turns fifty-five) into a lump sum savings calculator with an assumed interest rate of 6 percent per year, which is reasonable if she invests in a balanced

10 "Actuary Life Table: Period Life Table, 2017," Social Security, accessed February 5, 2021, https://www.ssa.gov/oact/STATS/table4c6.html.

portfolio of stocks and bonds. Turns out, if she starts saving and investing around $66,000 per year, she will have another $1.9 million by the age of fifty-five. Add that to the $350,000 she has in liquid assets now, and she'll have just over $2.25 million!

With a net income of $160,000 and fixed expenses of $50,000, Emma believes that she can certainly save $66,000 per year by cutting down on her excessive discretionary spending.

THE LESS YOU SPEND NOW, THE LESS YOU HAVE TO SAVE TO BECOME FINANCIALLY INDEPENDENT

By deciding to reduce her spending rate now, Emma is greatly reducing the length of her journey to financial independence. If Emma decided that she *had* to continue spending $150,000 per year, I would have told her that she needed to accumulate a lump sum of *at least* $3.75 million to achieve financial independence—and accumulating that amount would have been nearly impossible for her so long as that spending rate continued to be close to 93 percent of her post-tax income.

Emma was lucky in other ways, too—it was relatively easy for her to reduce her spending rate, being single with no dependents and having relatively low fixed expenses. For many others, reducing spending significantly is incredibly difficult to accomplish. It's much easier to avoid overspending in the first place than it is to reverse it once you're used to spending a given amount.

Even after reducing her spending, $2.25 million is the minimum, and I mean the *absolute minimum* Emma should aim to accumulate in order to reach a place of financial independence given her desired lifestyle. However, at that point, I don't recommend that she completely stop working forever. Why should she keep working, even part time, after she hits her goal? Well, she won't have a lot of cushion if she truly means to spend $90,000 per year for the rest of her life. Barring outside sources of income or wealth, she'd be cutting it pretty close, especially if her expenses unexpectedly rise or she lives much longer than another thirty years.

What I recommend for people like Emma is that they either aim to accumulate a net worth that is higher than this bare minimum, so that they have a *sizeable* cushion on top of the minimum net worth before they stop earning an income, or that they take a more moderate approach to living from that point on. Instead of retiring, why not just slow down? Continuing to have some income—any income—for longer gives you wonderful flexibility and financial security.*

*For me, followers of the FIRE movement demonstrate this point quite well. As author Jared Dillian put it: "Here's a quick summary of the FIRE movement: Living in deprivation for fifteen years so you can live in deprivation for fifty years."

And this seems to be true for many FIRE adherents. In addition to living in deprivation, which many accept as part of that lifestyle, most of those who completely retire also find themselves living stressfully close to the edge in terms of cash flows, because they save *just enough* to completely retire, per the 4 percent rule. Unfortunately, costly unexpected events can throw their carefully planned cash flows entirely off, putting them in a real jam. Also—and this is just my opinion based on watching many people retire—total retirement is not all it's cracked up to be for many people (especially energetic people). Having a purpose is crucial for happiness and mental well-being. This is something to ponder when considering whether total retirement would really make you happier.

After some thinking, Emma came up with a wonderful plan. Once she accumulated her minimum liquid net worth goal of $2.25 million, she would leave her consulting job and work as a ski instructor, likely making around $30,000 per year. Assuming her projected lifestyle cost of $90,000 per year at this point, this $30,000 in annual income will give her great financial security. It reduces her needed draw from savings to between $60,000 and $70,000 a year; a very sustainable withdrawal rate of between 2.6 percent and 3 percent of her $2.25 million lump sum.

I should also note that for many, Emma included, it's possible that she will have other sources of future assets and income beyond what she directly saves and earns for herself. For her in particular, the most likely sources of additional income would be Social Security and a modest inheritance from her parents. However, while she may get some monthly Social Security benefit at some point (which would be great since she's been paying into it her entire working life), it's certainly not a given. Neither is the inheritance—*nothing* is a given.

I encourage Emma, and all millennials, to ignore *all* possibilities of future income from outside sources when estimating what *minimum* lump sum needs to be accumulated for financial independence.

Is this extreme? Yes. But the benefits of planning this way far outweigh the potential downfalls of ending up reliant on outside sources for future financial security. This way, any future income from outside sources, is merely a bonus. If you go forward relying on others to hand you money decades from now, you risk ending up just like the baby boomers.

As you can probably tell, this is not an exact science. And that's okay. We don't need to be exact if we're conservative. Even if it was an exact science, the projection would soon lose relevance because the output would be based on inputs we have as of this exact moment in time. In reality, the world and our lives change drastically over time, and we have *a lot* of time ahead of us.

If the future is anything like the past, then it's a certainty that there are many unknowns ahead of us, many of which we can't possibly foresee. From a macro perspective, we have no idea what the world will be like decades from now, and the possibilities are endless. Our lives have already been marked by multiple events no one really foresaw: the rise of the internet, 9/11, the global financial crisis of 2008, and the global coronavirus pandemic of 2020.

Who knows what the future holds? Life expectancies might rise dramatically for any number of reasons. Maybe we finally cure cancer. Maybe someone will invent an expensive pill you can take to extend your life. The future world economy might be unrecognizable from that of today. We don't know what impact technology and AI will have on labor markets. We don't know what the tax code will look like, what inflation will be, or whether Social Security and other government benefit programs continue to exist as we know them.

We also have no idea what the future holds from a micro perspective. Take Emma, for example—she has no idea how long she'll actually live, or whether she'll be physically able to ski for decades more, or whether caring for a sick parent will require her to move elsewhere.

But there's one thing we do know, almost for certain. Having a lot of money is helpful for living a better life, in almost any scenario. That's been true throughout the past, and it's pretty likely to remain true in the future. So whatever the future holds, you'll be better off if you put in the work now to become wealthy and financially independent.

STRATEGIC CASH FLOW PLANNING

Alright, so at this point, you've:

- Done some deep thinking and answered the Kinder questions to solidify what you want out of life and how that should inform the qualitative aspects of your financial goals.
- Used the 4 percent rule as a guidepost to clarify the quantitative side of your financial goals.
- More specifically, you've come up with a net worth target to shoot for in your quest for financial independence.

Now, you need to roll up your sleeves and do the real work of charting a course to get there.

Goal-based cash flow planning is one of the most powerful and effective tools in your wealth-building toolbox.

At its core, it's your strategic plan for *how* you're going to live within your means. How will you allocate the resources at your disposal to most efficiently build your net worth? To put it simply: what are you doing with the money you make, and how can you be smarter about where you put it?

Being thoughtful and deliberate with your cash flows is vital for young accumulators who want to build wealth. Being lackadaisical about where your money goes can mean missing opportunities as a best-case scenario and avoidable financial catastrophes as a worst-case scenario. The potential upside to making the effort to plan from early on is massive—and the risks of not planning are equally massive.

SPENDING VS. SAVING

A well-known financial planner named Michael Kitces made the point that most cash flow-based financial planning advice starts with a savings rate, often based on the client's age: "You're twenty-five years old, so you should save 10 percent of your income," for example. Or, "You're thirty years old, so you should save 15 percent."

The problem with this kind of advice is that it's not actionable for many young people because, for them, their savings rate is not a decision in and of itself. Rather, it's the result of a bunch of spending decisions. Their savings rate is simply a function of what's left over at the end of each month or year. This is especially true for people with a lot of debt, people who live in areas with a high cost of living such as coastal cities (as many millennials do), and people with lower to middle incomes who don't make enough to have even 15 percent left over for savings after living expenses.

If you're in this situation, for whatever reason, you should focus on decreasing your spending rate first, rather than on setting or increasing your savings rate. Your spending rate is something over which you probably actually have some control.

Once your spending rate is low enough to leave you with a *good* amount of discretionary income at the end of every month or year, then you can decide how best to allocate that income.

By "*good* amount of discretionary income" left over, I mean:

- At least 15 percent if you're in your twenties.
- At least 20 percent if you're in your thirties and are just starting out on your wealth-building journey.

And note that I said *at least*. These are the *minimum* appropriate savings rates for people in their twenties and thirties. Your prudent savings rate may be higher, depending on your specific circumstances and goals.

If you're already at the place where you have enough discretionary income left after all your fixed expenses—the things you *have* to pay, like your housing and other mandatory bills—that it would be easy for you to save an appropriate minimum amount for your age, you can jump ahead to the savings rate section. (Though you may still find it useful to take a look at where the rest of your money is going!)

If you're not quite there yet, the following discussion of spending rate is for you. Ultimately, the goal for everyone is to be able to increase their savings rate, but I want to be realistic about the steps it takes to get there.

BUILD YOUR NET WORTH BY FOCUSING ON YOUR SPENDING RATE

Your spending rate is simply the result of the amount you spend divided by the amount you make. If setting a savings rate of 15 percent to 20 percent (or more) of your income feels impossible for you, then reducing your spending rate may be more actionable as a jumping-off point for cash flow planning than starting out by setting a savings rate. If you are in this category of people, you're in good company. This is where most young earners find themselves.

Your goal should be to reduce your spending rate enough to get you into the second category of people (a much smaller group), those who have substantial discretionary income available to save at the end of each month.

There are three main ways to get there:

1. Reduce your spending to reduce the rate of spending relative to your income.
2. Increase your income while not increasing your spending.
3. Increase your income while also reducing your spending.

Obviously, number three is the most powerful way to reduce your spending rate and will help you achieve your goal of moving on to increasing your savings rate faster.

I'm only going to cover in depth ways to reduce spending; I'm not going to discuss ways to increase your income because that's very individualized and there are plenty of resources on that elsewhere—but I will say that increasing your income is very powerful for wealth building and is essential for most low- to moderate-income people who wish to build wealth.

So how can you reduce your spending?

First, focus on the big things rather than little stuff. In most cases, it's the larger, more expensive categories of spending like transportation and housing that make the most dramatic difference in spending rates. Cutting back on small things—what some people call "the latte factor"—like dining out and takeout coffee does not meaningfully move the needle for most people when it comes to cutting back on spending.

> **Kaleb Horton**
> @kalebhorton
>
> Alright, I did the math. If I stopped eating avocado toast every day, I would be able to afford a bad house in Los Angeles in 642 years.
>
> > FOOD & DRINK
> >
> > **Millionaire to Millennials: Stop Buying Avocado Toast If You Want to Buy a Home**
> >
> > Jennifer Calfas
> > 12:45 PM ET
> >
> > Freely spending on avocados — the pricey, popular superfruit beloved by young people — may be one of the reasons why some young people can't afford a house, according to Australian millionaire and property mogul Tim Gurner.
>
> 11:35 AM · May 15, 2017 · Twitter for iPhone
>
> **6.7K** Retweets **303** Quote Tweets **15.2K** Likes

Take out your findings from the Personal Financial Audit exercise in chapter 2 and look at where your money goes. If you're like most people, a large portion of your spending goes toward the big stuff like housing and transportation. Not many people spend a small portion of their money on where they live and a massive amount of their income on coffee and avocado toast. And I really don't like the idea that saving money means you can't have the small pleasures in life; I think that's a problematic school of thought that's unhelpful and unhealthy. In my opinion, depriving yourself of life's little pleasures is not sustainable for a long period of time and is likely to lead to frugality fatigue (the phenomenon by which striving to be overly frugal causes you to snap and throw the budget out the window).

It's much simpler to make a couple of big decisions to reduce your spending rate by living in a less expensive home or driving a less expensive car than it is to make a thousand little decisions that deprive you of the small joys in life. The baby boomer generation wasn't wiped out in 2008 because they bought too many lattes but because they were underwater on their mortgages. Think about how many people you know who drive luxury vehicles but claim that they can't afford to max out their 401(k) every year. It just doesn't add up!

If you honestly evaluate your spending and see that you are spending a large proportion of your income on these smaller things, and you can reasonably cut back to move the needle on your spending rate in a meaningful way, then absolutely do so. But for most people, it's far more realistic to find a way to spend even just a few hundred dollars less per month on housing and transportation, so you can begin to save that difference in spending. Think about it—if your goal is to reduce your spending by $400 a month, are you more likely to find that in one or two large pieces of your budget or to cut back on 100 coffees a month?

In other words, you don't have to sweat the small stuff if you can move the needle on the big stuff. My dad likes to say that when it comes to choosing where you live, anything beyond a couple of rooms with a roof, a door, and a bathroom becomes a quality of life decision. This is also true of the car you drive, the clothes you wear, the wine you drink, and many other spending decisions. I love to remind myself of this when I catch myself thinking that I *need* something more luxurious than what would satisfy my basic needs. I didn't *need* to buy a bigger home this year, but I chose to do so because it enhances my quality of life—and that's a fine enough reason to spend money on just about anything *if* you can afford to do so while continuing to live within your means to build wealth.

If you're in the situation where you need to first figure out how to decrease your spending rate before you can focus on setting a reasonable savings rate, you're going to have to figure out the details of just how you do that yourself. There is no good cookie-cutter answer here; your solution depends on your particular goals and circumstances. But by conducting a personal financial audit (particularly focusing on step 1, confronting your financial reality, shown in chapter 2), you will be able to see exactly where your money goes and decide for yourself whether and where it's possible for you to cut back. If it's not possible to cut back at all, you should consider reducing your spending rate by increasing your income.

Once you start allocating resources so that you have substantial discretionary income left over after fixed expenses, congratulations! The hardest part is over. You are now in the position to move on to setting a savings rate and using the strategies I'll discuss in the next section.

BUILD YOUR NET WORTH BY FOCUSING ON YOUR SAVINGS RATE

If your spending rate leaves you with at least...

- 15 percent left to save if you're in your twenties
- 20 percent left to save if you're in your thirties and just getting started on your wealth-building journey

...then further congratulations are in order! You have ample discretionary income to save in the first place. You are living well within your means, and now you can start saving to build wealth.

When I say "living within your means," I mean spending a good amount less than you make. This applies whether you're putting extra cash down on debt, which I consider to be a form of saving, or you're setting money aside for the future.

Debt elimination is essential to building a positive net worth and achieving financial independence. I'll discuss whether you should prioritize allocating cash towards saving/investing or debt reduction a little later in this chapter. For now, just know that living on less than you make over a long period of time is the surest path to financial independence.

> Paying down debt counts as saving for these purposes, with one caveat: If you have significant debt of a kind in which payments do not build positive equity in an asset—this includes all student debt and most consumer debt—you should aim for an even higher savings rate if possible.

I recommend that you set a non-negotiable savings rate, one you can stick to. Then plan the rest of your spending around that. By setting your savings rate first and sticking to it, you can have peace of mind spending whatever is left over.

From here, the two strategies I recommend for building your savings rate are: one, automating to pay yourself first; and two, saving part of every raise.

AUTOMATE TO PAY YOURSELF FIRST

I highly recommend setting up an automated system to pay yourself first on a regular, consistent basis. Paying yourself first means that *you* are the first bill that you pay every month. Many people wait until the month or year is over to see what's left to save. Don't do that. Your income should funnel into savings or debt reduction before it goes anywhere else.

It's easy to do, one less decision you have to make, and one less item on your to-do list. Plus, it goes a long way towards reducing the temptation to spend more than you should. If your income automatically gets siphoned off towards various savings vehicles, it's more likely to be "out of sight, out of mind." In a way, it's like you never had it.

This strategy is a no-brainer. It reduces friction and makes building wealth much less stressful. It also sets you up to live within your means by default.

But how should you divvy up where your automatic savings go? Well, that depends on what your specific savings goals are—and your particular financial situation—but if you're funding a cash goal like an emergency fund or a down payment on a house, you should simply have an automatic monthly transfer from your main checking account into a separate savings account. If you're saving toward retirement and have an employer-sponsored retirement plan, that's easy to automate—just fill out the paperwork authorizing your employer to automatically withhold a percentage of your pay from every paycheck, which then goes straight into your retirement account every month. If you're self-employed or funding your own retirement account, you can also automate that funding in basically the same way.

A note for people with inconsistent cash flows: If you're a freelancer, small business owner, or anyone else with an inconsistent income, it's even more important for you to live within your means and save aggressively. You, too, can automate to pay yourself first, but it will take more thinking and doing than it would for someone with a steady, predictable income.

Setting and sticking to a non-negotiable savings rate is especially key for you. My recommendation is that you first have a very large cash cushion or emergency fund so you're not left in the lurch if income dries up for some time. Having this will go a long way towards you being able to make plans for other savings goals. You can save for this by making the decision to automatically funnel some percentage of all take-home income to that fund.

Once you have that, you can easily automate, via direct deposit, a percentage of incoming cash flows into a self-employed retirement plan (you have multiple options) or on paying down debt.

SAVE PART OF EVERY RAISE AND BONUS

The next strategy for increasing your savings rate, which you can do concurrently with the first, is to save part of every raise and bonus you receive.

I realize that not everyone is in the position to expect regular raises or bonuses. However, most of us do increase our incomes, one way or another, throughout our twenties, thirties, and forties. And if you are in a position where you can expect pay raises and/or annual bonus income, you are in luck because this gives you a wonderful opportunity for automated wealth building.

Too many people pre-spend anticipated additional income. Commonly, people do this with bonus money, planning ahead to spend it all on unnecessary consumption before it's even received (or worse, actually pre-spending on consumption). This is very easy to correct—just don't do it. Going forward, plan to send at least half (more if you're willing) of every bonus towards savings.

Deciding now to save at least half of every future raise is a very simple and powerful way to avoid dangerous lifestyle creep. Lifestyle creep is a very common, sneaky, and damaging phenomenon whereby you increase your lifestyle expenditures over time, usually in step with an increasing income. This is especially common earlier in your career when you are presumably earning less and/or paying off debt. It's really easy for this to get out of control and continue long past the beginning stages of your career without ever realizing it. To paraphrase Hemingway, people go bankrupt gradually and then very suddenly.

You should be able to get an idea, by conducting your Personal Financial Audit from chapter 2 and doing some personal reflection, whether you've fallen into a pattern of lifestyle creep. If you have, *stop now.*

I've seen many people increase their lifestyle spending in step with their income—and that's how some baby boomers ended up in trouble, under-saved and financially dependent for the rest of their lives. In fact, I know a single lawyer who makes $400,000 a year and *still* lives paycheck to paycheck. This is a guy who happily lived on $120,000 per year less than a decade ago when he started out his career in the public sector and was able to afford everything he needed. Back then, he saved around $12,000 per year, a savings rate of 10 percent.

Just several years later, he has a higher private sector income—and the lifestyle to match. He managed to more than triple his income but hasn't budged on his savings rate. Now, his $12,000 per year amounts to a 3 percent savings rate, and he's used to spending a lot more money. There is no way his 3 percent savings rate will ever be enough to build him a net worth high enough to achieve financial independence.

Think how much wealth he could build if he had started saving half of every raise earlier in his career!

OTHER CASH FLOW PLANNING CONSIDERATIONS

Once you're saving to build wealth, you have some decisions to make about where exactly to allocate your savings.

If your income is sufficiently high, this part may be easy because you're able to do it all. But if you don't have enough income coming in to fund all of your goals at once, at least not initially, this decision-making process may involve some strategic trade-offs.

EMERGENCY FUND

Your first consideration should be your emergency fund. As the name implies, this is a cash pile you keep aside for emergencies such as a large, unexpected expense or drop in income. I cannot stress the importance of this enough. Without an emergency fund, even the best-laid financial plans can fly out the window at the first unexpected event or job loss. As we learned in 2020, sh*t happens. We should expect this and be prepared.

Your emergency fund should consist of somewhere between six and twelve months (or more) of your fixed expenses, and it should be in cash that you can access at a moment's notice. It should be readily available to you but also segregated from the rest of your money. Fully funding this should be your number-one financial priority. If you don't have an adequate emergency fund, automate to pay into this first and don't divert your cash anywhere else until it is fully funded.

Exactly how much *you* need in your emergency fund depends on factors that vary for each individual.

The less stable your job or income, the larger your emergency fund should be. If you're an independent contractor for example, with large gaps between paydays, you should have enough cash to cover you for months of fixed expenses, plus enough for an unforeseen emergency. If you have people who depend on your income for food, shelter, and other basic necessities, you should have a larger emergency fund. Some people, especially enthusiastic investors, don't like sitting on "too much" cash, knowing that they can get a better return on dollars invested in the markets. Others can't sleep at night without knowing that they have a very large cash pile sitting around.

A good exercise for coming up with an appropriately sized emergency fund for you is to run through various what-if scenarios that would count as emergency financial situations:

- What if I lost my job and couldn't find employment for an extended period of time?
- What if my partner lost his/her job for an extended period of time?
- What if I (or a financial dependent) needed to pay for a large unforeseen expense, like a medical bill, car, new roof, etc.?

If you're a young professional in great health with a stable income, no financial dependents, and proper insurance coverage, then you're probably fine with an emergency fund on the smaller side. (In chapter 7, we'll look at how being properly insured helps cut against the need for a larger emergency fund in some scenarios, like disability or liability.)

As I write this, we are in the midst of dealing with the COVID-19 pandemic and the ensuing economic instability. With high unemployment and general economic insecurity, the importance of having an emergency fund, a safety cushion for unforeseeable events just like this, is all too clear.

DEBT VS. INVESTING

Once your emergency fund is taken care of, you need to decide where to funnel the rest of your savings. I like to visualize cash flow planning as having a bunch of buckets you can pour your money into. Once your emergency fund bucket is full, that cash can flow somewhere else.

COLD, HARD CASH

Despite everything I just said about how important it is to have enough cash to carry you through the rough times, you should understand that cash—straight-up cash—is not productive. If you are in the habit of keeping cash beyond what you need for your emergency fund and upcoming expenses, you should know that your money could be put to much better use. I'll go into more detail in chapter 5, when we talk about investing, but just know that beyond having your basic operating expenses and your emergency fund, your *extra* money should always be working for you—not sitting in an account doing nothing.

It should either be making a guaranteed return by paying down debt, or it should be invested for a long-term return in the stock market. I often see people who have a lot more cash than they need for an emergency fund, when they could be paying down debts or saving for retirement. That is a surprisingly common missed opportunity.

An exception to this is if you have a savings goal that requires cash, like a house down payment.

Many people have multiple buckets they're trying to pour money into all at the same time. Strategic cash flow planning is really just figuring out which buckets to fill, with how much, and in what order.

Like so much in financial planning, those buckets are completely individualized. But some common buckets include: student loans, mortgage, credit cards or other consumer debt, a down payment fund, pre-tax retirement accounts, a Roth IRA or other after-tax retirement accounts, and education savings plans for young children.

A very common question that comes up in this regard is whether to prioritize extra cash towards debt reduction or towards investing for the future.

In purely monetary terms, the best strategy for answering this question comes down to finding an arbitrage. Can you earn more money by investing cash than you will by using it to pay down the debt in question? For example, if you have debt financed at a 3 percent interest rate and you can likely make 7 percent on average by investing for the long term in the stock market, then you're better off putting your extra cash towards investing—again, in purely monetary terms. If you're dealing with higher interest rate debt, it becomes less likely that you can get a return higher than the interest you're paying on that debt; in that case, you'll come out ahead by prioritizing debt reduction over investing.

Some scenarios in this regard are fairly straightforward, but others are not. For those situations, I have a simple thought matrix to help with your decision:

1. If you have debt, does it bother you? Does it keep you up at night? If you answered yes to this question, *focus on paying down debt first.* Some people are very debt averse. I work with many clients who can't even bear to have a low interest mortgage on their home. If having debt stresses you out, you should prioritize debt reduction over investing—even if it doesn't make strict monetary sense. Other advisors might say that I'm wrong, that you should set aside your feelings and do what makes most fiscal sense, but I think peace of mind is priceless. I myself am very debt averse, so I understand the stress involved—and I don't think that's any way to live if you feel the same way. Overall, the goal is to be happy and independent. (You'll find solid strategies for debt reduction in chapter 4).
2. If you answered no to the first question—having debt doesn't bother you—then the next question is whether the debt is at a low interest rate. If you have debt with an interest rate of 4 percent or less, it most likely makes sense for you to prioritize *extra* cash towards investing *wisely*, in a disciplined way, into a balanced portfolio of stocks and bonds (beyond making your regular, minimum debt payments). Over the long term, you're likely to make a return higher than 4 percent by investing this way (more on this in chapter 5!), so this is a situation where you

can comfortably focus on investing over paying down debt—if you're comfortable doing so. *However*, total debt elimination is still a prerequisite to financial independence and should be part of your financial plan.

3. If, however, you're paying down debt with an interest rate above 4 percent (and refinancing to a lower rate doesn't make sense or isn't possible), then you're probably better off putting all of your extra cash down on the debt, with the goal of paying it down as quickly as possible. Once you get over 4 percent with interest rates, it becomes much less certain that you will "do better" by investing your extra dollars in the stock market. In contrast, every dollar you put down on debt at 5 percent interest has a guaranteed 5 percent return.

The only caveat I have to this whole matrix is that if you have an employer-sponsored retirement plan and it has a match, which is common for people who work for large companies, then you should contribute enough to that plan to get the full match. Why? Because that is *free money*—and free money doesn't come around very often. (We'll look at this concept in more detail in chapter 6.)

As you zero out debts, reallocate the cash that you were putting towards debt payments toward savings (including extra payments on other debt)—in the same way you automate to pay yourself first and save part of every raise. I know that it's tempting to shift newfound cash flows towards lifestyle spending, but you'll do best to keep your eye on the ball: a net worth high enough to give you true financial independence.

WHAT IF IT'S NOT JUST ME?

Personal financial planning is just that—highly *personal.* Money is a flashpoint for many couples, and fighting over money is one of the leading causes of divorce in the US. So what should you do if you and your partner just don't see eye to eye when it comes to money?

This is a common problem, one that can be helped by self-awareness and education—for *both* people—and by talking with a good financial planner who can act as an objective third party and voice of reason. Unfortunately, there's not always a right or wrong answer; personal financial planning is full of grey areas. But a financial planner can look at your situation without emotion and give advice from a purely monetary perspective. Sometimes, knowing what makes the most sense, objectively, can at least be a jumping-off point for discussion and compromise.

I personally find that returning to George Kinder's three questions (see the opening section of this chapter) is very likely to help couples refocus on what they have in common and what's most important in life.

While these questions can be uncomfortable, and it can be difficult to look at them, they get at what's truly important to you—not the things we just think we have to say are important. Looking at these questions, whether by yourself or as a couple, can help you zoom out to see what money is for, what your life is about, and how you can use money to have a fulfilling life without regrets.

If your situation is truly dire, and you and your partner are in a state of deadlock, you might consider seeing a financial therapist. Financial therapy is a relatively new field within personal finance that further explores the emotional side of financial decision-making.

BESPOKE ADVICE

I am laying out a general framework here. It's not meant to be cookie-cutter, one-size-fits-all advice. When it comes to the nitty gritty parts of personal financial planning, cookie-cutter advice simply doesn't work. Every one of us is unique, and so are our financial lives. You will have to look at your life and make decisions about what is prudent for you to do given your unique circumstances. At the end of the day, it's your money.

I've had many clients ask me to tell them what they can and can't spend money on, but I'll never do that. I learned that from my dad, who says, "What you spend your money on is not my business. I don't care if you want to spend all your money on rubber duckies, as long as you save the amount we've agreed on."

I'm not going to tell you that you can't get manicures, go out to dinner, or take vacations. It's up to you to figure out where you are, where you'd like to end up, and exactly how you're going to get there. That self-knowledge, combined with the personal finance education and wealth building framework I lay out in this book will give you *your* recipe for financial independence.

If you've done the work up to this point, you should have an idea of how much you need to save to reach financial independence, and how you can use cash flow planning to get there. And if you are focusing on paying down debt as part of your savings plan, let the next chapter be your guide.

LET'S BREAK IT DOWN

- You probably need to accumulate more than you think to reach financial independence. For most of us, our target net worth should be in the millions.
- There are qualitative and quantitative aspects to financial goal-setting. You can use the Three Kinder Questions, developed by George Kinder, to home in on the qualitative aspects of your financial goals and the 4 percent rule as a basis for calculating the net worth you need to accumulate to achieve them.
- Once your goals are set, strategic, goal-based cash flow planning is one of the strongest tools you have for achieving them.
- You can accumulate your target net worth by increasing your savings rate. If you are in your twenties, you should be saving at least 15 percent of your gross income. If you are in your thirties, you should be saving at least 20 percent of your gross income. If you are not currently in a position to save at least 15 percent to 20 percent of your income, then you should focus first on reducing your spending rate.
- Two strategies for increasing your savings rate are: using automation to pay yourself first and saving half of every raise (and/or bonus).
- Building an emergency fund with at least six months of fixed expenses in cash should be your first cash flow planning priority. Once you have that, you can move onto focusing on debt reduction and investing to build your net worth.

CHAPTER 4

DEALING WITH DEBT

The information in this chapter is incredibly important, and I don't want to bury the lede so I'll start out with this: debt is a wealth destroyer. It should be avoided at all costs—*especially* the truly problematic forms of debt, which include basically all consumer debt and student loan debt that is not sure to pay for itself with a much higher resulting income. If you have problematic debt, paying it down quickly should be your top priority (after accumulating an emergency fund).

That's the chapter in a nutshell. Read on for the details.

Danielle and Raul are friends of friends. When I met them at a friend's birthday dinner, they were newly minted physicians fresh out of residency. Used to making $60,000 per year as residents, they'd just quadrupled their incomes and were full of excitement about the future.

Between the two of them, they had $800,000 in student loan debt from attending private undergraduate and medical school programs. With an expected combined income of $500,000 per year and a baby on the way, they were excitedly discussing how they'd just been approved for an $800,000 mortgage and were planning to make an offer on a house in a neighborhood with great schools.

I was floored. I happened to know that Danielle and Raul had basically nothing in the way of assets, being fresh out of training. It was pretty clear to me that this couple had never done the simple math to arrive at the fact that they were one transaction away from being nearly $1.6 million in the hole. It wasn't my place to comment on their financial decisions in that setting, but I couldn't stop thinking about how much they might regret starting out their careers and family so very far from ever reaching financial independence. They'd have to pay off $1.6 million just to get to a zero net worth. On top of that, they'd likely be trying to pay for childcare, save for college, and save for retirement, in addition to paying for everyday life expenses.

Like I said, they weren't asking for my advice. If they had, I would have advised them to delay the home purchase and to keep living like residents for just a few more years. If they could find a way to continue living on $120,000 together and threw all their extra newfound cash flow down on their student loans, they could greatly reduce their student loan balance in a very short period of time. And, as we'll discuss below, they'd save a ton of money on interest by paying the loans down quickly. Just this one small choice—which would mean a few more years of living in the exact manner to which they'd become accustomed—would vastly improve their long term financial stability and help them move much closer to financial independence.

THE TRUE COST OF DEBT

Debt is typically a result of someone else lending you money to pay for something you couldn't otherwise afford.

Some debt can be useful, sure. You can use debt to buy an asset that might appreciate, like a house, or to finance an education that will give you the ability to earn a higher income. A loan to start a small business, which might increase your net worth, can be a good thing. When used reasonably, debt can be a useful tool for actually increasing your net worth in the long term.

A lot of debt, however, is not reasonable. Most other debt, especially debt used to finance consumption or a depreciating asset, is almost always a bad idea. While the positive compounding interest on your stock investments causes the underlying balance to grow over long periods of time, debt interest also compounds to allow your owed balance to grow over time. Debt can become disastrous, working against financial independence and decreasing net worth exponentially.

Most debt comes at a cost, and the cost of borrowing should always be understood by the borrower, but it rarely is.

Let's go back to Danielle and Raul, the couple whose story opened this chapter, and look at the actual, *true* cost of their debt. It's not just borrowing $1.6 million and paying back $1.6 million.

If we assume normal interest rates—an average of 7 percent on the student loans with a ten-year repayment term and 4 percent on a thirty-year fixed-rate mortgage—and we assume that this couple doesn't make any extra payments on either loan, the interest costs will be $314,000 on the student loans and $575,000 on the mortgage. That means interest costs of $889,000—in addition to the $1.6 million in principal for both loans. *That* is the true cost of their debt. All told, they'll *spend* nearly $2.5 million in total for their degrees and their home.

Don't get me wrong—I'm not saying that financing education or a home is a bad thing! In fact, in many cases, it's a wise decision. I *am* saying that you should know and understand the true cost of debt you take on ahead of time, no matter the situation. This knowledge is essential to any analysis of whether taking on that debt might enhance or destroy your chances of building wealth.

In the next section, I'll discuss a few more basic concepts you should understand about debt, whether you already have it or are considering taking it on.

BASICS OF DEBT, EXPLAINED

In the simplest terms, *debt* is money that you owe to someone else. The amount of money borrowed is called the *principal* of the loan.

Lenders take on risk when they lend people money to buy things those people otherwise couldn't afford, the largest risk being that the lender will not be paid back on time or in full. To compensate lenders for taking this risk, they charge borrowers a fee on the borrowed money, called *interest.* Interest is the cost of borrowing money, and it's usually expressed as a percentage of the loan amount.

You'll frequently see interest expressed as an *annual percentage rate*, or APR. The *interest rate* is the fee charged for borrowing the principal. The *APR*, which is almost always higher than the interest rate, usually includes other fees and costs of borrowing, so it more accurately reflects your total cost of borrowing.

ALL ABOUT INTEREST

Interest rates vary and can fluctuate based on a variety of

factors. Some of these factors are out of your control, such as market movements and lender policies. Lenders tend to charge higher interest rates when they perceive higher risk associated with the loan or borrower.

For example, secured loans—loans that are secured by an actual object of value that the lender can repossess if you don't pay your debt, like a car or a house—typically have lower interest rates than unsecured debt. Unsecured loans, such as student loans and credit card debt, typically come with higher interest rates because the lender doesn't have the recourse of recouping their money by taking an asset if you stop paying.

Lenders also generally charge higher interest rates for loans with a longer repayment period, loans to a borrower with a low credit score, and for loans where the amount borrowed is a high percentage of the value of the asset it's attached to (in the case of secured debt). This is especially true in the private-loan market and in the home- and auto-loan markets.

For you, the higher the interest rate, the more expensive the borrowed money is. You'll occasionally come across zero-interest loans, typically for financing consumer purchases like cars or Peloton bikes, but those are typically only zero interest for a finite period of time before they start incurring interest. Be aware of that and read the fine print if you come across one of these loans.

Interest rates can also be fixed or variable for many types of debt. Fixed rates are just what they sound like—the interest rate charged on the loan is established at the outset and remains the same for the entire repayment term, so the payments are also the same each month. With variable rate loans, the interest rate on your loan can fluctuate with market interest rates.

Borrowers who choose a variable rate instead of a fixed rate are making a bet that interest rates will decline in the future, while the lender is hoping that rates will go up over time. Initial interest rates for fixed-rate loans are usually higher than for variable-rate loans because the lender is accounting for the possibility that market interest rates will be raised after you lock in your rate for the long term.

With variable-rate loans, the borrower runs the risk of interest rates rising during their repayment period. For this reason, I rarely recommend that people consider variable-rate loans unless they are absolutely certain to repay their loan over a very short period of time—no more than a few years.

Types of Interest

Interest works differently for different types of loans.

There are two types of interest: simple interest and compound interest. Compound interest means that you pay interest on the principal balance of the loan as well as the interest that was added to the principal balance in prior periods. Basically, this means that you pay interest on top of interest and it can compound exponentially.

With simple interest loans, you pay interest on the principal only. Naturally, these are much easier to reduce than compound interest loans. Most auto loans, mortgages, and student loans are simple interest loans, whereas most credit cards charge compound interest, which is why credit card debt is the most dangerous and expensive way to borrow money.

I have a friend, for example, who's up to her ears in credit card debt—which, in her case, has an average interest rate of 24 percent that's compounding daily—but she's prioritizing paying off her car loan, with simple interest at only 5 percent. She will save thousands upon thousands of dollars by prioritizing pay-down of the higher and compound interest credit card debt over the lower and simple interest auto debt.

Generally, I believe that the Avalanche method is the best strategy for paying down debt. This method prioritizes complete pay-down in the order of highest to lowest interest debt. So, for example, if you have:

- $85,000 in student loan debt at 6.8 percent.
- $420,000 in home mortgage debt at 3.5 percent.

- $9,000 in credit card debt at 18.5 percent.

You should focus on eliminating these debts in this order: 1) credit card, 2) student loans, then 3) home mortgage.

LOAN TERMS AND AMORTIZATION

So yes, interest rates have a massive effect on the total amount you pay overall. The length of your repayment term also affects the amount you pay, though the concept is much simpler: the faster you repay the loan, the less you'll pay overall. This is the case with amortized loans, such as most home, auto, student, and personal loans.

With an amortizing loan, you make regular, preset payments of a fixed amount for a defined period of time—the repayment term. Part of each payment goes to repaying the principal and the rest goes to paying interest. Interest payments are typically front-loaded so that a higher percentage of each payment goes towards interest in the earlier portion of the loan repayment term. The percentage of each payment that goes towards interest decreases over time until the interest is paid off, at which point each payment goes mostly to paying down the principal balance of the loan.

Loans with longer repayment terms have lower monthly payments because you're spreading out the payments over a longer period of time. However, they cost more overall because interest accrues for a longer period of time. Conversely, loans with shorter repayment terms have higher monthly payments but are less costly overall due to the decreased time you are paying interest on the balance.

It's very important that you understand this trade-off, but few people think of loans in these terms. Many people tend to look only at the monthly payment when assessing affordability of a loan. It's so important to also know and consider the total amount you'll pay over the entire period of the loan.

For example, let's look at the same $700,000 fixed rate mortgage loan at 4 percent but with three different repayment terms:

1. If the loan is repaid over thirty years, the borrower will make monthly payments of $3,341, and pay $503,086 in interest costs, for a total outlay of $1,203,086 to zero out the loan.
2. If the loan is repaid over twenty years, the borrower will make monthly payments of $4,241, and pay $318,046 in interest costs, for a total outlay of $1,018,046 to zero out the loan. That's a savings of $185,040 over the thirty-year loan, despite the higher monthly payment.
3. If the loan is repaid over fifteen years, the borrower will make monthly payments of $5,177, and pay $232,006 in interest costs, for a total outlay of $932,006 to zero out the loan. That's a savings of $86,040 over the twenty-year

loan and $271,080 over the thirty-year loan, despite the higher monthly payments.

So, while the thirty-year loan may look much more affordable than the fifteen- or twenty-year loans when you only consider the monthly payment, it's actually far more expensive in reality.

MAKING EXTRA PAYMENTS

If you pay more than your minimum payment amount in any month on an amortized loan, the additional dollars will go towards reducing the principal balance on the loan, thus moving you down the amortization schedule and reducing the interest and overall amount you will pay.

If the borrower with the thirty-year fixed rate loan from above regularly paid an additional $500 per month, starting in year five of the loan, they shave five years off the loan repayment term, resulting in interest savings—and therefore overall savings—of $82,439. Rather than paying $1,203,086 to zero out the loan, they'll pay $1,120,647 total.

If, however, they start making the same extra payments from the very beginning of the loan repayment term, they'll shave six years and seven months off the repayment term, resulting in a paid-off mortgage in just over twenty-three years and a savings of $123,862.

Of course, the higher the extra payment amount, or the sooner it starts, the shorter the repayment term, and therefore the greater the savings.

As I mentioned, mortgages, auto loans, student loans, and most personal loans are amortized, and work in this way. Credit card debt on the other hand, is not amortized, as there are no fixed repayment schedules and interest continues to be charged on the interest, growing the balance of the loan exponentially. This is called revolving debt, which we'll get into a little later in this chapter.

In my opinion, reading about this concept only goes so far. The best way for you to understand how debt works is by playing around with online calculators. If you have debt, plug your specific figures into an online calculator. Run an amortization schedule over various repayment periods, and run an extra payments amortization schedule (just google "extra payments calculator"). You'll quickly see what I'm talking about.

Online calculators are amazing resources. I recommend those by bankrate.com and nerdwallet.com, but there are a ton of others you can use to run various calculations and schedules for different loan amounts, interest rates, and loan terms to see the difference you can make by adding in extra payments, shortening the repayment schedule, refinancing to a lower interest rate, or simply borrowing less.

There's truly no better way to understand your specific situation.

TYPES OF DEBT

Now let's look at the most common types of debt millennials may encounter, starting with housing debt.

HOUSING DEBT

Most young people don't have the assets to buy a home without taking on some debt. Mortgages are a well-accepted necessity among young buyers for this reason. Plus, when you finance a home purchase, the assumption is that you'll build equity in the home, which increases your net worth. Your home equity is just the value of your home (what you could sell it for), less any loans on the house. Home equity builds, or increases, 1) when you pay down your mortgage, and 2) when your home appreciates in value. Because you never *truly* know the exact value of your home on any given day, you almost never know *exactly* how much equity you have in your home. But you can get a rough estimate by subtracting your loan balance from the assumed fair market value of the home.

How Much House Can I Afford?

A quick rule of thumb about how much house is right for you: you can afford to borrow far less than your lender will give you. Many people fall into the trap of buying way more than they can afford, ending up "house poor."

The 28-36 rule is a great little rule of thumb young accumulators can use to answer the question of, "How much house can I afford?" This rule says that:

1. A maximum of 28 percent of your monthly gross income should go towards *all housing costs*, including principal, interest, taxes, and insurance (PITI); and
2. A maximum of 36 percent of your gross monthly income should go to debt servicing overall. For example, if you have student loans or a combination of other debt and those debt payments make up 15 percent of your monthly gross income, you know that your total housing costs should use no more than 21 percent of your monthly gross income.

Again, this is just a rule of thumb, and it's not the only guideline or rule of thumb in the personal finance sphere that sets out to advise young people on this topic. But I like it for its simplicity, and wide applicability, so I recommend following those guidelines.

You may consider 28 percent of your gross income way too much to spend on housing—I get that, especially considering that taxes may eat up close to 35 percent or more of your remaining gross income. If you save 20 percent of what's left after that, you only have 17 percent for other fixed expenses and discretionary spending. You may feel house poor in that scenario—and it wouldn't jive with my lifestyle either—but life is all about trade-offs. This is a personal decision, and within those maximum parameters, you'll have to decide what's best for you.

Also remember that the buying process and all it entails is frequently much more expensive than people assume. If you're considering buying a home, you should have enough money for a down payment, furnishing or renovation costs, and closing costs, which can be very high—usually in the five digits—while still having a cash cushion that's separate from your emergency fund. And don't forget that you should still be able to continue to put at least 15 percent to 20 percent of your income towards building your wealth by saving, investing, or reducing other debt! (If this doesn't sound familiar, please re-read the section about savings rates in chapter 3.)

Don't fall into the situation where you start to accumulate credit card debt (the most evil kind of debt) immediately after taking out a big mortgage for a home purchase because you've depleted all your liquid savings. That's a recipe for disaster.

If this sounds impossible, I can relate! As I write this, my husband and I are getting settled in our newly purchased home in the DC area. We've been urban renters for a long time, so this is a big deal for us! Plus, with a baby on the way, we have an entirely new slew of anticipated expenses coming down the pipeline. It's *a lot*, but no one ever said that building wealth is easy! It takes patience and discipline.

Renting vs. Buying

The New York Times has an amazing calculator that can help you answer the question, "Should I rent or buy?" in purely monetary terms. If you're considering buying a home, you should definitely run your numbers through that calculator.

Renting gets a bad rap. If I had a nickel for every time I heard someone say, "Renting is flushing your money down a toilet!" I'd be very wealthy indeed. But as you may see when you check out *The New York Times* rent-versus-buy calculator, you'll see that the topic is much more nuanced than most people realize. There are many variables that go into the analysis of which is a better deal—again, in purely economic terms.

Many people who compare the costs of renting versus owning only look at a monthly rent payment versus a monthly mortgage payment. If the mortgage payment is lower, as it often is, they conclude that renting is a terrible deal—but this is misguided.

The true costs of ownership are much higher than most people realize. A mortgage payment is just one part of the cost of owning your own home. You also have to consider the costs of buying and reselling, property taxes, insurance, delayed maintenance and repairs, and on and on. The total cost of homeownership in the US averages out to 8 percent to 10 percent of the home's value each year over long periods of time. If you talk to almost any long-term homeowner, they'll tell you that their actual overall cost of ownership on an average annual basis far exceeds just the monthly mortgage payments. If you're planning to buy a home, it's essential that you consider the true cash outlay required to buy, own, and maintain the home (not just the cash required to pay the mortgage).

There are lots of pros and cons of both homeownership and renting. There's no black or white, "correct" choice between the two in general. What's "correct" really depends on each potential buyer or renter's personal circumstances and motivations for buying or renting.

However, one of the most common arguments I hear people make in favor of homeownership over renting is that their home purchase will be a good investment. Sadly, this is commonly not the case for a few general reasons, especially when compared with a well-diversified investment portfolio of stocks and bonds.

First, you'd have to sell the roof over your head to realize the return on this so-called "great" investment. How inconvenient! Homes, relative to many other investment opportunities, are very illiquid.* If you have a net worth of $1 million, but $900,000 of it is equity in the roof over your family's head, would you feel financially independent? (The answer should be no.)

*This is also true of investment real estate such as rental homes, commercial real estate, etc.

Second, long-term historic returns on US residential real estate are between 1 percent and 2 percent a year after taxes and inflation. Yes, homes do tend to appreciate over long periods of time—but so do stocks! And 1 percent to 2 percent per year is not a *great* return, especially when you consider that the S&P 500 has a historical average return of 7 percent per year adjusted for inflation.

Of course, there are exceptions here—hot markets, good timing, luck, etcetera usually play a role in that. But making a great return on the home you live in is the exception, not the norm.

However, that doesn't mean there aren't lots of other great reasons to own your home!

Monetarily, a huge benefit of owning is that your monthly mortgage payments help you build equity, which adds to your net worth. You also get to benefit from any appreciation on the home. Mortgage payments stay fixed (unless you have a variable loan), so they tend to become more and more affordable over the life of the loan due to inflation. Plus, mortgage interest, and some amount of property tax, is deductible. Finally, having a paid-off home goes a long way towards achieving and maintaining financial independence.

But the decision to buy a home is not usually based on purely monetary considerations. There are also qualitative benefits to homeownership. For example, my husband and I decided to buy, after renting for many years, because we felt that there would be a psychological benefit to "putting roots down" somewhere before we started our family. We also wanted more space and to be able to decorate as we pleased. In some ways, we also enjoy being our own landlords and cutting out the bureaucratic nonsense we dealt with for years while living in an apartment building owned by a large corporate management company.

On the flipside, taking out a mortgage means decreasing your net worth, at least initially. If you're able to rent for a lot less than buying and you invest the difference in the stock market, you'll probably come out ahead in purely monetary terms over the long run.

And on the qualitative side, renting gives you more flexibility to take a job across the country or to move if your neighbors are terrible. Many people love the freedom that comes with renting and truly enjoy *not* putting roots down. Additionally, *you* don't have to pay to replace the water heater or AC when it inevitably breaks.

Again, this analysis is highly nuanced, so you have to decide what's right for you. Using an online rent-versus-buy calculator should go a long way towards seeing what makes sense for you, monetarily at least. But be cautious (regardless of what an online calculator says)—you absolutely should not buy a home if doing so will make you cash-poor or derail you from your path to building a positive net worth that will one day afford you financial independence.

STUDENT LOANS

Taking on student loan debt, within reason, can boost your net worth by increasing your earning power. However, as we all know, many people today (millennials in particular), find themselves in an intractable student loan predicament. The student loan crisis has become a hot button topic in recent years, and so far, those in power haven't found a good solution—though everyone has an opinion on what *should* be done.

Meanwhile, many millennials who are actually dealing with massive student loan burdens feel hopeless, angry, anxious, depressed, and resentful. Bright-eyed and bushy-tailed, they took on student loan debt in the optimistic pursuit of higher education, which would in turn provide a great career path that would provide an income sufficient to repay the student loans *and* build a prosperous future.

Yet today's reality is that everyone's screaming about the ridiculously high interest rates on student loans and the insanely overinflated cost of higher education. There's now extreme awareness amongst most generations that financing higher education with high-interest, non-dischargeable loans does not necessarily lead to better financial outcomes—and in fact, for many, it does not pay off at all. But this level of awareness around the dangers of student loans just wasn't there in the earlier 2000s, when many millennials were taking on debt to get degrees.

So, if you're a millennial in a difficult student loan predicament, what are you to do? Sure, you could wait around and hope for the government to pass some kind of massive forgiveness program, but that's a very dangerous bet. Even if something was passed, how likely is it to be as all-encompassing and fabulous as politicians today promise on the campaign trails? If you have student loans and you're serious about someday attaining financial independence, you can't wait around for the government to solve your problem. You must take matters into your own hands. You must take control.

I have encountered many young professionals who say that their student loan situation makes them feel completely hopeless. These people tend to have two things in common: 1) a large student loan burden and 2) a passive approach to paying off the loans. They feel that they have no control over the loans and therefore their own financial futures. They mostly cope with this terrible feeling by trying to forget that the loans exist. They make regular minimum payments and attempt to focus their thoughts, and extra money, on happier causes.

But try as they may, these people are not happy. And they're further setting themselves up for the very financial failure they so dread. Despite their best efforts to repress thoughts about their debt troubles, the loans hang over their heads like dark clouds, always lingering there in the background.

If you are in this predicament, I have good news for you: You have other options. Which option is best for you, I can't say. That depends on your personal circumstances and goals. But I can tell you that you need to proactively investigate the details of your specific student loan situation (if you haven't already) and do the work to explore all of *your* repayment options in detail.

Once you decide on a strategy for moving forward, pursue it with vigor. Track and continually evaluate your progress. I assure you, this active and intentional approach will have a far better outcome than the passive, "I try not to think about them" approach.

So, what are your options? They can be grouped into three major strategies:

1. Attack and (maybe) refinance.
2. Lower your payments.
3. Pursue forgiveness.

I'm going to discuss these three options *very* broadly here, because there's so much nitty-gritty detail involved with all the sub-options of each, and I couldn't possibly do it all justice here.

I encourage you to take this as a broad overview—a framework for thinking through the big picture of problem solving for student loan issues—and delve much deeper into the specifics on your own. An amazing resource I recommend for this is studentloanhero.com. This site has information on every possible student loan repayment scenario, presented in an organized and coherent way, and includes multiple calculators and quizzes you can use to evaluate options given your specific circumstances.

Attack and (Maybe) Refinance

The first option is to attack your student loans and to possibly refinance them.

This, in my opinion, is the most widely applicable repayment strategy for student loan borrowers, and it's simple. Attack your student loans with everything you have. Make extra payments whenever possible, with the goal of paying them down as quickly as possible. Make lifestyle changes, if necessary, to maximize the amount of cash you can throw down on the loans. If you're able to make more money through a side income or second job, do it, and use the cash for extra payments. The standard repayment period for federal (and many private) loans is ten years, or 120 payments. Make it your goal to eliminate your debt in less time than that. Remember, these are amortized loans (just like a home mortgage), so every extra payment you make shortens the repayment period, reducing the interest you pay, and therefore the amount you pay overall.

If you have federal or private loans, I strongly encourage you to consider refinancing at some point to reduce your interest rate. Interest rates on private and federal student loans are typically quite high—6 percent or more—and it's likely that you'll be able to get a lower rate by refinancing a few years into your repayment term (and possibly again a few years after that). At the very least, get refinance quotes from a few lenders every couple of years.

If you're able to refinance to a lower interest rate, your overall repayment amount will lower, and you'll be able to get to zero even faster if you continue to attack the balance. This approach is one of the surest ways to regain control and eliminate your loans so you can move on to building wealth.

You may opt not to refinance if you have federal loans, because doing so means giving up some of the protections and options afforded to federal student loan borrowers, including forgiveness and income-driven repayment plans. That's a reasonable decision, but it does mean sticking with the higher interest rates and paying a higher amount overall unless you make extra payments and pay the loan down faster than the standard repayment period.

There's a real mental benefit to actively eroding a student loan balance, and it's self-reinforcing. Momentum is the key here—once you get going, you can watch your balance drop lower and lower, which activates your mental reward center and motivates you to keep at it.

One of my clients is a physician named Brian. In 2016, he came to me with $399,000 of student loan debt at 6.5 percent interest. I've helped him refinance twice to get lower rates—first with SoFi to 5.62 percent. After making payments for a couple years, he was able to refinance his remaining $322,000 balance into a five-year, fixed-rate loan at 3.71 percent—almost half of his original interest rate! We did the math and found that he is going to save over $100,000 in interest alone.

I've seen many people take this approach, despite facing obstacles and hardships along the way, and I can tell you, they are much happier and much better off financially, than the passive approach people. More about them below.

Lower Your Payments

If you have federal student loans, there are multiple options available for reducing your monthly payment lower than it would be under the standard ten-year repayment program. These options, collectively referred to as Income Driven Repayment (IDR), include multiple repayment plans that will lower your monthly payment to some amount between 10 percent and 20 percent of your discretionary income and extend your repayment period to a term of twenty or twenty-five years. At the end of the repayment period, your loans are forgiven. However, the forgiven amount is taxable to you in that year.

This is my least favorite approach. I know a lot of people who are on these repayment plans, and most of them feel to some degree helpless and hopeless about their student loan situation. I get why. Rather than proactively eroding their loans, they're passively making minimum payments. This will be their situation for the next twenty or twenty-five years. Meanwhile, the interest is compounding on their remaining loan balance, causing it to continually grow even larger. And that tax bill at the end is due in full upon forgiveness—and it can easily be tens of thousands of dollars.

It's no wonder they feel like they will never get out from under their loans! Having student loan debt for two decades or more is completely antithetical to the concept of building wealth and becoming financially independent.

I don't recommend this strategy, and I urge you to avoid it if at all possible.

Pursue Employment-Specific Forgiveness

There are multiple student loan repayment help and forgiveness options available to workers in specific fields: the military, public service, healthcare, teaching, law, and more. If you work in a field where a specific repayment help or forgiveness plan is available to you, I encourage you to explore it. Note that most of these programs offer to pay some set or limited amount towards your student loans in exchange for your commitment to work in a specific field for a set period of time. For example, lawyers who work for the Department of Justice for at least three years may receive up to $60,000 in loan assistance through the DOJ's Attorney Student Loan Repayment program.

The most widely applicable and comprehensive program in this sphere is Public Service Loan Forgiveness (PSLF), which is available to public service workers in a wide variety of fields. This is available to people who:

- Have federal student loans, and
- Work in a qualifying job full-time for ten years while enrolled in the PSLF program,
- While making 120 on-time consecutive payments during that period.

Of course, to maximize forgiveness, it makes sense for participants to lower monthly payments as much as possible, usually by enrolling in one of the Income Driven Repayment (IDR) plans.

And, unlike forgiveness under the traditional IDR plans, the forgiven balance is not taxable. It almost sounds too good to be true, right?

Well, for some people, it was. The program started in 2007, so the first participants became eligible for forgiveness in 2017. Some were then told that they were not eligible for public service loan forgiveness for a variety of reasons—improper paperwork, bad assumptions, seemingly changed rules, etc. Needless to say, these people got screwed. They were left with a large accumulated loan balance—still in need of repayment—after ten years of making minimum IDR payments under the assumption that the rest would be forgiven.

Still, others have had success with this program, which is a fabulous option when it works out. If you're eligible for this, I recommend exploring it. But I would only enroll and make lower than standard monthly repayments if I was absolutely certain that I qualified for PSLF (get it in writing) and was *certain* to remain qualified for ten consecutive years.

A Word of Warning

If you don't currently have student loans but are thinking about taking them out, make sure that you know the true cost of borrowing.

Run an amortization schedule with an online calculator and learn *exactly* how much you'll end up spending on your degree—principal, interest, and all.

Once you know what the degree will truly cost you, ask yourself how likely it is that getting the degree will help you attain an income high enough to repay the loans within a reasonable period of time so you can move forward on your path to financial independence. It probably doesn't make sense, for example, to borrow $200,000 to pursue a degree that will land you in a field where you're likely to make less than $90,000 a year.

Just something to consider before committing yourself to loan repayment for the next decade or more!

AUTO LOANS

Paying interest on debt to finance the purchase of a depreciating asset such as a car is a terrible idea. You know how people like to say that a car loses 30 percent of its value the minute you drive it off the lot? Well, it's not far from true—new cars really do start depreciating when you drive them off the lot and will continue to do so, losing 20 percent to 30 percent of their value by the end of the first year of ownership. Most cars then continue to depreciate 15 percent or more each year through year six (as opposed to homes, which tend to increase in value over long periods of time).

When you take out a loan* to pay for a car, you end up spending more money to own the car than the car is worth at any point in time, including on the day you buy it, while the car simultaneously loses value.

> *Zero-interest loans are an exception, and they are plentiful these days. I have no problem with financing a car purchase with a zero-interest loan—it's free money! But *be sure to pay the entire balance down during the zero-interest period.* Once that's over, the interest rates jump up.

Both Edmunds and Kelley Blue Book have calculators for figuring out the true cost of owning a vehicle—and these calculators will blow your mind. They factor in all the smaller aspects of car ownership that people tend to forget, things like insurance, taxes and fees, maintenance and repairs, fuel, financing, and depreciation. Using these calculators, you can see that the true cost of owning a car over a five-year period is always much higher than the purchase price.

But I acknowledge that most of us want a safe, reliable way to get around. So what's a prudent way to buy a car? If you are very wealthy, then you should drive whatever you want. If you're not, consider buying an inexpensive new car and driving it until the wheels fall off. Alternately, you can buy a used car and drive it until the wheels fall off. As you can see from the Edmunds or KBB calculators, the first three years of ownership are the most expensive time to buy a car, so buying a two- or three-year-old car will save you a lot of money—money that you can invest or put down on debt to make a positive return.

You may be wondering, "But what about leasing?" Leasing rarely makes financial sense.

Here are the few, *limited* scenarios where leasing might make sense for you:

1. You are very wealthy and like to drive a different new car every few years—have at it!
2. You're in a profession where it's very important to drive a decent new car for good optics (realtors come to mind).
3. You find a lease deal where the total lease cost is less than the cost to own the same car over the same period of time (use a calculator to figure this one out). Aka: a good deal. These come along from time to time.

Outside of these scenarios, I can't think of a situation where leasing makes good financial sense. When you lease a car, you're paying to drive it during the most expensive years of its existence.

CREDIT CARD DEBT

Using credit card debt to finance depreciating assets (most things you would buy with a credit card) or consumption that you otherwise cannot afford is very dangerous. Spending money on credit cards that you do not pay off in full every cycle is *by far* the most expensive way to borrow money.

Most credit cards have annual percentage rates of 18 percent to 25 percent, which compounds daily. That means that, each day beyond the due date for the payment of those charges, the lender charges you interest on the balance. The next day, they charge interest on the new, larger balance, and then again the day after that, and so on. This is why credit card debt is so difficult for people to overcome. Once the compounding interest gains momentum, the balance explodes. And credit card debt is not amortized like home mortgage loans, student loans, or auto loans. There are no set payment or loan amounts—as long as you stay within your credit limit, you can keep borrowing.

Now, don't get me wrong—I'm a fan of credit cards. I have multiple, and I love participating in the rewards programs. My husband and I are able to purchase a few flights and hotel stays every year solely with accumulated credit card points. But that comes with a big caveat: we pay our balance *in full* every month. Doing so helps us build credit, and it's the only prudent way to use credit cards.

If you have high-interest credit card debt, which is most credit card debt, getting rid of it should be your top debt pay-down priority over all debt. It makes no sense to focus extra cash towards student loans that are at 6 percent interest while you have credit card debt compounding daily at 18 percent.

> I (of course) recommend using online calculators (Bankrate, Credit Karma, NerdWallet) for viewing scenarios of how credit card debt compounds, how long it would take you to fully pay a balance making only minimum payments, and how much sooner you can pay your balance down by making larger payments.

If you're in this position, one option you can explore is opening a credit card with a zero percent APR and transferring the balance of all your existing credit cards to that account. Once you do so, the interest will stop accumulating, making it easier for you to attack the balance. Be aware, though, that most zero-APR cards jump up to higher interest rates after one year, so you're likely on a strict timeline for payoff.

Another option is to get a fixed-rate personal loan to consolidate and pay off the credit card debt. Interest on personal loans is typically lower than interest on credit cards, and it's simple interest instead of compound interest, as I discussed earlier in this chapter. Because the interest is only charged on the principal balance, pay down becomes much easier.

A third option would be to negotiate with your credit card lender. In some cases, they'll work with cardholders to lower rates or work on repayment schedules. It's worth asking if they can help!

One final word on credit card debt: If you tend to spend more than you can afford, then you should not have credit cards, period.

A FINAL WORD ON FINANCING

For those who wish to achieve financial independence, there are only two ways to approach debt: avoidance and reduction. Of those two, debt avoidance is far more powerful.

Of course, total avoidance isn't possible for most young accumulators. But we should absolutely avoid unnecessary and problematic debt at all costs. As I mentioned in the beginning of this chapter, that means basically all debt outside of a reasonable home mortgage and student loan debt.

If you have problematic debt, paying it completely down, in the order of highest to lowest interest loans, should be your top priority after accumulating a sufficient emergency fund. Don't take a passive approach. Attack your debt with disciplined, strategic cash flow planning (see chapter 3). If you do this, you'll be well on your way to financial independence.

ARE YOU SWIMMING NAKED?

Danielle and Raul, the young couple with $1.6 million in student loan and housing debt from the beginning of this chapter may seem unrelatable because they're such an extreme example, but middle class America is full of examples of how debt taken out to finance even average lifestyles can add up very quickly, with terrible outcomes.

Warren Buffett has a great line, "Only when the tide goes out do you discover who's been swimming naked." It so perfectly describes the dilemma of under-saved and overleveraged people who run into unexpected financial strains.

We saw this play out in 2008, and we're seeing it again with the economic fallout from the coronavirus pandemic in 2020, particularly in the middle class. And it had been a long time coming—at the start of 2020, middle-class Americans had been loading up on debt for years to live well beyond their means, without much worry. The amount of non-housing debt owed by American families making over $98,018 in pre-tax income increased by 32 percent, adjusted for inflation, between 2004 and 2016.[11]

But at the start of 2020, the economy was booming, incomes were rising, and the stock market was eleven years into a

11 AnnaMaria Andriotis, "No Job, Loads of Debt: COVID Upends Middle-Class Family Finances, *The Wall Street Journal*, September 20, 2020, https://www.wsj.com/articles/covid-unemployment-debt-middle-class-family-finances-11600122791?mod=hp_lead_pos8.

historic bull market. What could go wrong? As per usual, everything was good—until it wasn't.

As I was editing this chapter of the book, I was also reading article after article about how the economic fallout from the coronavirus pandemic affected overleveraged white collar workers. A September 2020 *Wall Street Journal* article titled "No Job, Loads of Debt: COVID Upends Middle Class Family Finances," reported on multiple anecdotal examples of middle class families struggling under the burden of their monthly debt obligations as they experienced pandemic-related income reductions.

In one example, a forty-three-year-old New York attorney named Alyse and her husband were used to making $175,000 per year together, but they experienced a drop in income when the courthouses closed and Alyse could no longer continue her typical work. Unfortunately, they had $9,000 in monthly debt obligations. This included: $3,000 per month in mortgage payments, $750 per month in car payments, $680 per month in payments for a personal loan to renovate a bathroom, and $800 per month in student loan payments.*

*The article did not detail what made up the rest of the $9,000 per month in debt payments.

Suddenly, they found themselves scrambling to stop the bleeding—pausing car payments, asking for a break on the personal loan, and deferring student loan payments. The article mentions that they managed to pay their mortgage by using money they'd set aside for their daughter's summer camp.[12]

What does this all tell you?

1. This family clearly did not have an emergency fund. If they did, it wasn't sufficient. With debt obligations alone costing them $9,000 per month, I think we can safely assume that additional fixed expenses might cost at least another $2,000 per month. This necessitates an emergency fund of *at least* $66,000 in cash, set aside for just this sort of situation.
2. This family was *way* overleveraged. Their monthly debt obligations take up over 61 percent of their pre-COVID *gross* income. Take out likely taxes for a NY couple in their tax bracket, and there's not much left. No wonder they didn't have an emergency fund—they were likely living paycheck to paycheck. And it's also likely they don't have much in the way of any additional savings for the future.
3. Unlike Raul and Danielle (again, the $1.6 million in debt couple from the beginning of the chapter), this couple probably isn't financing any one thing that would seem outrageous at first glance. Each individual loan, in and of itself, probably seemed reasonable when they took it

12 Ibid.

out. But one day they woke up and realized they were in way over their heads. This is a very easy (and common) trap to fall into.

This sad story of white collar financial mismanagement was just one of many detailed in the abundance of news articles on this topic in 2020.

I feel terrible for this family, and the many others like them. They are not totally to blame for their financial woes. Who could have predicted the pandemic and the ensuing fallout? I sure didn't. But that's exactly why we should all be financially prepared for the unknown. We see, time and time again, that sh*t happens—on a macro scale, like the pandemic, and on a micro-scale, like a personal disability or random job loss. This family was just one bad event away from a potential bankruptcy for years—it just happened to be the pandemic that got them.

And that, in a nutshell, is why debt is so very dangerous.

But you can save yourself, starting now. Once you've paid down your debt, you're ready to increase your saving—and investing. The next chapter will help you add sound investment advice to your financial plan.

LET'S BREAK IT DOWN

- Debt is a wealth destroyer that should be avoided at all costs. Especially the most problematic kinds of debt, which include basically all consumer debt and student loan debt that does not pay for itself with a much higher resulting income.
- If you have problematic debt, eliminating it ASAP should be your top priority after filling up your emergency fund.
- When used reasonably, debt can be a useful tool for increasing your net worth over the long term. However, you should have a firm understanding of the *true* cost of borrowing before taking on debt.
- The true cost of borrowing is the total amount you will spend to repay the loan—including repayment of principal *and* total interest paid.
- Interest is the cost of borrowing money. The higher the interest rate, the more expensive the borrowed money is.
- Debt that does not build positive equity in an asset, such as all consumer debt and most student debt, should be prioritized for pay-down in most cases.
- Financing the purchases of depreciating assets (such as cars and consumer items) with debt is guaranteed to lose you money, and should be avoided.
- If you wish to achieve financial independence, there are only two ways to approach debt: avoidance and reduction. Of those two, avoidance is far more powerful.
- In most cases, the Avalanche method is the most prudent debt reduction strategy: pay down loans in order of highest to lowest interest rate.

CHAPTER 5

INVESTING

DISCLAIMER

Many books have been written about investing, and I only have one chapter to dedicate to it here. So, I'm going to keep this *very* high level, and I'm going to focus on the investing topics that I feel are most crucial for the average millennial to understand. Due to limited space here, I've tried to avoid going either too basic (e.g. what is a stock) or too "in the weeds" (e.g. the intricacies of derivatives trading). If you'd like to learn more about investing in general, or about any particular type of investing, there are thousands of resources available for you out there, and I encourage you to dig deeper!

Imagine that someone gifted a younger you $20,000 in cash on January 1, 1990. If you parked that cash in a typical checking account that paid .04 percent per year and never touched it again, you'd have $20,241 on January 1, 2020. So, you made $241. Not bad, right?

Not so fast. While it looks like you made money, you actually lost a lot of purchasing power. As we all know, $20,000 buys a lot less in 2020 than it did in 1990. In fact, $20,000 in 1990 dollars is equivalent to roughly $40,000 in 2020 dollars, so you have actually lost half of your purchasing power while "playing it safe."

To further illustrate the point: In 1990, the average cost of a new car was $9,437. In 2020, the average cost of a new car is $38,948. That $20,000 would have afforded you 2.1 average new cars in 1990 and only around 0.51—not even one—average new car in 2020. Not good!

Now, let's assume that you immediately invested your $20,000 into an S&P 500 stock index fund back on January 1 of 1990 and never touched it again. Come January of 2020, the value of your investment would be over $195,000.*

*This is assuming that you reinvested dividends. You can use this historical investment calculator to play around with other scenarios: https://financial-calculators.com/historical-investment-calculator.

INVESTED IN YOUR OUTCOME

We all know that investing comes with a certain amount of risk, especially when done in a foolish or speculative way (which it frequently is). But keeping your savings in cash over long periods of time also produces the absolute loss of purchasing power. Why? Two reasons: inflation and taxes. Inflation is the silent but steady force that erodes the purchasing power of your dollars over time. Taxes, well you probably know all about that! (And if you don't, they're the topic of our next chapter.)

You've probably heard your parents talk about how a gallon of milk cost forty-five cents when they were ten, or how they only made two dollars an hour at their first summer job in the seventies. The difference between that forty-five-cent gallon of milk and the four-dollar gallon (or more!) you're buying now is due to inflation—the gradual increase in the prices of things over time—and it also explains why a dollar buys less and less over time.

Inflation is typically subtle and gradual, which is why it feels less pronounced for us than it does for our parents—we haven't been around long enough to experience it to the same degree. But, absent exceptional economic circumstances, we're also likely to experience the same continuous erosion of the value of our dollars by inflation over the years. As I write this in 2020, inflation is running at just over 2 percent per year on average and has been for the last two decades. That means that by 2030, we can reasonably expect a dollar to buy almost 20 percent less than it did in 2020.

And, as I mentioned, taxes are the other reason the same

amount of cash doesn't have the same purchasing power it did a few decades ago. Taxes will be assessed in various forms on any income you make over any time period—even if the "gains" just keep up with inflation.

These two factors are the reasons why when you invest you need to make returns that cover both the erosion of taxes and inflation over time just to avoid losing money and purchasing power.

And this is why I'm going to stick my stake in the ground and say that for most millennials, the best and easiest way to cover the costs of taxes and inflation (plus enjoy some true gains) is through a strategy of long-term, buy-and-hold investing into a diversified portfolio of mostly stocks. And you should be doing so now if you aren't already.

WHY STOCKS—AND WHY NOW?

For the average non-professional millennial investor, putting savings into a diversified portfolio of stocks (and maybe *some* bonds) is your best strategy for making a return on your saved dollars above taxes and inflation.

WHY STOCKS?

Stock market returns vary drastically from year to year. But if you zoom out, the US stock market (as measured by the

S&P 500) has returned around 10 percent on average over the last 100 years. Take out 2 percent to 4 percent on average per year for inflation and taxes and you're still looking at a "real" return of 6 percent to 7 percent per year.

The historical positive return on stocks is largely due to the power of compounding gains and interest, which we touched on in the last chapter when discussing the devastating effects of compounding interest on debt. However, in the case of stock investing, the compounding effect works in your favor. In fact, Albert Einstein is thought to have said (and whether he actually said this or not makes it no less true), "Gravity isn't the strongest force in the universe; compound interest is."

Here's a simplified example of how compounding gains and interest works in the case of straight buy-and-hold investing, which is what I recommend:

Let's say that you invest $10,000 into a portfolio of stocks that earns a return of 7 percent per year* and let that initial investment sit. In the first year, you'd earn $700. In the second year, you'd earn 7 percent on the $10,700 you had at the end of the first year, making your balance $11,449 after the second year, and so on. By the tenth year, you'd have $19,672. By the twentieth year, you'd have $38,697. And all of that growth happened with you doing absolutely nothing at all after the initial investment.

*This isn't totally realistic, as no stock consistently earns the exact same return year after year, but you get the point.

This snowball effect becomes magnified with larger invested sums. Essentially, the more you have, the more you make. I've witnessed the miracle of compounding gains in large accounts, and it's truly something to behold. Once you have a large enough sum invested (do I even have to clarify that I mean invested *well*), it's likely to become a growth monster that compounds exponentially over the years with no action from you. In fact, in nearly all cases, it's much better if you actually *don't* take any further action. More on that in a bit.

WHY NOW?

As I've mentioned, time is one of the greatest resources we have as millennials, and this is especially true when it comes to investing. The sooner you start investing, the longer your invested dollars have to grow by compounding gains on gains. This is why a dollar invested in the S&P 500 in January of 1970 would have had a cumulative return of *3,529 percent* in January of 2020.

Over shorter periods of time, stocks can be volatile, with dramatic swings up and down. But, over longer periods of time (meaning decades, not just a few years), stocks almost always go up. The more time you have, the more you can afford to tolerate the shorter-term swings in prices, which means you can put more into higher returning stocks (versus lower returning yet "safer" asset classes like cash or bonds).

For an under-saved baby boomer approaching retirement, it's really too late to take *full* advantage of this wonderful, passive way to build wealth—but it's not too late for us. While the deck seems stacked against us in some ways, time is on our side. If we use it wisely, we *can* overcome the unique financial obstacles the universe has laid at our feet to become prosperous and financially independent.

BUT, SERIOUSLY, WHY *STOCKS?*

Is stock investing the only way to make a long-term return above taxes and inflation? No. I'm not denying here that there are other investment strategies that people successfully use to build wealth every day. But I would argue that these other ways are perhaps riskier, harder, and less common.

You may be wondering *why not real estate investing? Why not crypto? Why not commodities or derivatives trading?*

If you're already reasonably knowledgeable about any one of these alternative investment strategies (and you *really* know what you're doing), then by all means, go ahead. But I've found that most millennials (and most people in general) are simply not that knowledgeable in these areas. In fact, many of the young investors I come across who think they are sophisticated crypto/real estate/alternatives investors are really of the "actually know just enough to be dangerous" variety. And if you don't *really* know what you're doing, these strategies present too much risk and, in many cases, illiquidity, for them to be reasonable venues for your life savings relative to stocks.

I'll elaborate a bit on real estate in particular because I'm frequently asked about investing in rental houses, vacation houses, commercial space, land, and more. I believe that there are rare times when these are good investments, especially for the average millennial with finite cash available for investing.

One's home is a quality of life issue, not an investment in most cases (see chapter 4 for more explanation). Even very desirable home property tends to appreciate, at best, at around the rate of inflation nationally.

Other real estate is rarely a good investment. One reason is that it's relatively illiquid. It can be hard to sell, and frequently takes a long time to offload, even in the best of circumstances. If the property has or develops environmental or structural problems, this further compounds the illiquidity. Also, external events can act against the property. Think of home prices in 2007 through 2011 in most locales. Now think about owning rental real estate in one of our major US cities throughout the 2020 global pandemic.

In addition, real estate buildings carry multiple ongoing costs, regardless of the price you can sell them for. There's insurance, property tax, scheduled repairs, expected large capitalized expenses (roof, A/C), and unexpected damage and repairs (termites, storm damage, etc.).

While long-term investing in global stocks can reasonably be expected to return roughly 7 percent a year over the long term, the real estate investment with all its risk and illiquidity should be expected to return, at minimum, a double-digit return. Yet, most that I see do not even come close.

Plus, if you're just interested in having some exposure to real estate as an asset class, you can do that in a much more liquid and diversified way by investing in real estate mutual funds and ETFs. Bottom line, you must be quite knowledgeable, quite lucky, and/or quite involved to do well enough in real estate (or crypto and other alternative strategies) to compensate you for the added risk and relative lack of liquidity.

Building a basic, low-cost, *highly liquid* stock portfolio for the purpose of long-term buy-and-hold investing can be done by almost anyone—with little sophistication, little risk over the long-term, and with a near guarantee to make a decent enough return over taxes and inflation. The same cannot be said for anything else. I'll leave it at that.

> One exception I'd be remiss not to mention:
>
> If you're building your own business, it's expected—and not unreasonable—for you to plunge most (if not all) of your free cash back into your business. I can't disagree with that and encourage you to go forth and prosper. Of course, the goal is that you'll eventually have enough liquidity to diversify your wealth outside of your business holdings, but that's further down the road for most millennial business owners.

LET'S GET INVESTING!

So, what exactly do I mean by **long-term, buy-and-hold investing, into a diversified portfolio of mostly stocks?** Let's break it down.

LONG TERM

As we discussed in chapter 3, your first financial funding priority should be your emergency fund, which should hold at least six months of your fixed expenses in cash. In addition, you should have enough cash to cover ongoing operating expenses and any nearer term purchases that you need to buy with cash to avoid taking on debt (basically every purchase except for 80 percent or less of a home purchase).

If you're still accumulating enough cash to fill your emergency fund and cover ongoing and near-term purchases, investing is down the road for you. Money for these goals should be kept in liquid, safe vehicles such as cash, money market funds, and bank CDs. It should never be exposed to the short-term volatility of the stock market.

If your cash goals are funded and you have debts, then I advise you to revisit the Debt vs. Investing thought matrix in chapter 3 to come up with a plan for prioritizing future cash flows.

If, after all of that, you're in a place where you're able to start investing for the future, you should be doing so *only* with the intention that all of your invested dollars are to remain invested for the long term (a decade or longer). Over short periods of time—days, months, even a few years—stocks are volatile. They go up, they go down, sometimes by large amounts, sometimes by small amounts, but most importantly, these short-term directional movements are entirely unpredictable. 2020 is a wonderful example of this.

Over longer periods, however, stock markets* go up.

*Notice I said "markets" and not "individual stocks" or individual companies. Not all companies continue to go up over long periods of time, which is why diversification is so important. More on that below.

Not to beat a dead horse with the "time is on our side" bit, but this is yet another place where I feel it must be emphasized.

It's simple. Stock markets go up over long periods of time. As millennials, we have *lots* of time for invested dollars to grow and compound. The earlier we start, the longer our dollars can stay invested. The longer our dollars can stay invested, the more they will multiply.

BUY-AND-HOLD INVESTING

Dalbar, a respected investment research firm, has been publishing the leading study on investor behavior every year for over twenty-five years. Year after year, they find that the average investor underperforms the very markets they invest in, "in both good times and bad." In 2018, for example, the study found that the average S&P 500 investor lost 9.42 percent for the year, while the S&P 500 lost only 4.38 percent.[13]

This relative underperformance by investors is almost entirely

13 "Average Investor Blown Away by Market Turmoil in 2018," Dalbar.com, accessed February 5, 2021, https://www.dalbar.com/Portals/dalbar/Cache/News/PressReleases/QAIBPressRelease_2019.pdf.

due to *behavior*. We know that markets tend to go up over the long run. Average investors, however, don't just let their invested dollars sit and grow over long periods of time. Instead, they tend to buy and sell in and out of the markets in attempts to maximize their returns, frequently in contravention of the age-old adage "buy low, sell high." In fact, average investors on the whole tend to buy what's high and sell what's low.

As the Dalbar study shows, this always backfires. In reality, no one, not even among the "experts," has been shown to consistently and reliably outperform public markets by "timing" trades in and out. That's why *every* nonprofessional investor (and most professional investors) is better off with a strategy of **long-term, buy-and-hold investing.**

How do you pursue a strategy of long-term, buy-and-hold investing? It's as simple as it sounds: invest your dollars (more on *how* below) then do nothing for a *very* long time. That's it. Really.

There's no need for you to watch the markets closely or trade in and out in an attempt at being opportunistic. That is speculating, not investing—there's a difference. As Fred Schwed wrote in his classic investing book, *Where Are the Customers' Yachts?*, "Speculation is an effort, probably unsuccessful, to turn a little money into a lot. Investing is an effort, which should be successful, to prevent a lot of money from becoming a little."

Noted investor Benjamin Graham also hit the nail on the head when he said in his famed book, *The Intelligent Investor*, that "speculating when you think you're investing" is the most "unintelligent" thing you can do. As the Dalbar study shows, it's better if you just sit tight and let the markets do their thing.

And that's the beauty of this strategy—it has tremendous results, and it requires very little work or cleverness. In fact, the less you do, the better.

But *doing nothing* isn't always easy. It can be really hard, especially when the markets are volatile and there's a lot of fear or greed pushing markets in either direction. Or when there's mania or hype about a particular investment or sector. Or when it seems like "everyone is doing it," and your brother-in-law won't shut up about what a killing he's made trading Tesla, pot stocks, tech stocks, crypto, Beanie Babies, etc.—you get the gist.

I have three recommendations that will make it much easier for you to just do nothing:

1. **Ignore day-to-day financial headlines if possible.** If you must pay attention, make sure that you can do so in a

disinterested way. Stop if you find yourself reacting emotionally or considering making changes to your portfolio based on current headlines. You don't need to worry about current geopolitical events or who wins the midterms. You don't need to worry about whether "stocks rise on stimulus talk hopes" or "stocks fall on stimulus talk skepticism." None of this has any bearing on what stocks will be worth twenty years from now—and that's the ball you've got your eye on.

2. **Don't watch your investments too closely.** Psychology studies tell us that, for humans, the pain of losing is psychologically twice as acute as the pleasure of gaining.[14] This is called loss aversion. Stock markets close "down" one out of every three days even though they tend to go up overall. If you're a long-term buy-and-hold investor, why needlessly or repeatedly open yourself up to feeling the pain of loss when you know that the best plan of action is to do nothing?
3. **Ignore friends or family members who give you "hot tips."** The overwhelming likelihood is that these people don't really know what they're doing (despite what they may think) and are engaging in short-term-oriented, speculative behavior. While they may get lucky occasionally, this rarely goes well over the long term. Don't risk your hard-earned dollars by speculating on short-

14 Daniel Kahneman and Amos Tversky, "Prospect Theory: An Analysis of Decision under Risk," *Econometricia* 47, no. 2 (1979): 263-92, https://doi.org/10.2307/1914185.

term events when you're certain to do well in the end by doing hardly anything at all in the meantime.

Because markets go up, if you buy and hold for a long time, you will almost certainly buy low and sell high by default, a feat most average investors cannot seem to accomplish. Again, remember that $20,000 invested in the S&P 500 in January of 1990 would have turned into $195,000 by January of 2020 if simply left alone to grow.

Warren Buffett, a famous advocate for long-term, buy-and-hold investing, has said of his investment strategy at Berkshire Hathaway, "Our favorite holding period is forever," and, "Lethargy bordering on sloth remains the cornerstone of our investment style."

If you won't listen to me, listen to Warren!

INTO A DIVERSIFIED PORTFOLIO OF MOSTLY STOCKS

Before I end this chapter, I'd like to talk a bit about diversification, which has been described by Nobel Prize winner Harry Markowitz as "the only free lunch" in investing.

We already discussed why most millennials should be mostly investing in stocks. But I want to clarify that I do not mean picking individual stocks. No—stock picking is largely a fool's errand, especially if you're not a professional investor (and even then, it still is in most cases).

Instead, the average millennial should own broadly diversified stock mutual funds and ETFs that mimic the broader global markets, as well as some diversified bond funds. Why? Having a diversified portfolio reduces short-term volatility and long-term risk. It is one of the most essential and time-tested strategies for successful long-term investing. Put simply, it means not having all of your eggs in one basket.

When your portfolio is diversified, it means that you own assets across various asset classes, sectors, and industries that are ideally not correlated—meaning, they won't respond in the same way to the same events. This, of course, reduces the risk that everything in your portfolio will go down at the same time. It also means that most of the time, something in your portfolio *will* be down even when others are up. That's a good thing. If everything in your portfolio goes up at the same time, you're probably not well diversified.

The investment research firm Callan puts out a chart each year called "The Periodic Table of Investment Returns." I encourage you to look it up. It looks like a patchwork quilt of colored squares (a la the Periodic Table), with each color-coded square representing one of nine different asset classes, and each column representing the investment performance of all nine asset classes in a given year, listed in order of highest to lowest performing.

What you'll quickly see is that 1) a different colored square/asset class tops the list each year and 2) the entire order rearranges from year to year. For example, US large cap stocks topped the list only twice between 2000 and 2019. Emerging markets stocks topped the list five times over that same period with insanely high returns—but it also finished at the bottom four times. I won't go on; you really should look for yourself because it's a fabulous visual illustration of the benefits of diversification.

It takes discipline to stay diversified, just like it takes discipline to stick with a buy-and-hold strategy. In the last decade, for example, FANG stocks (Facebook, Amazon, Netflix, Google) have been the sexiest buy. They keep going up, and people keep buying more. It's tempting to follow the crowd and make a concentrated bet on these four tech stocks with the assumption that they will continue on this stellar trajectory forever. But they probably won't, not forever. And the odds that you or I will perfectly time an exit strategy are slim to none. Better to spread your money around so that no one particular company, sector, or asset class can bring down the whole ship.

A note on bonds:

Stocks and bonds have different purposes in an investment portfolio. Bonds are lower returning and less volatile than stocks, and they mainly serve to *preserve* your capital. Stocks, which are there for the purpose of capital *appreciation*, must "pay" you more to compensate you for the additional risk you take on by investing in a more volatile asset class. Holding both stocks and bonds greatly adds diversification to your portfolio, because they are traditionally non-correlated. For example, when stocks had a terrible year in 2008, bonds were relatively stable. However, this is not always the case—there have also been times where bonds and stocks have both gone down or up at the same time.

As I write this in 2020, it's very difficult to make any sort of meaningful return on bonds, especially relative to stocks. For this reason, I recommend that young investors who can stick with a buy-and-hold strategy put almost all long-term investment dollars into stocks.

Your asset allocation—the ratio of stocks to bonds in your portfolio—is one of the most important determinants of your long-term return. It matters even more than your selection of stocks and bonds within that allocation. However, there's no magical formula for what's the "best" asset allocation across the board; it really comes down to your personal risk tolerance—your ability to weather market downturns and volatility without losing too much sleep at night or making inopportune changes to your portfolio.

The average millennial investor who is just starting out will do well over the long run with an asset allocation that is mostly in diversified US stock funds, with some diversified foreign stock funds, and maybe a *small* allocation to bond funds. The lower your risk tolerance—again, meaning the more apt you are to be disturbed by stock market movements—the more bonds you should have relative to stocks. But know that the higher the ratio of bonds in your portfolio, the lower your long-term returns will be. This is why I recommend that most millennials be almost entirely in stocks, with an allocation to bonds only to the extent that you need that stability to "sleep at night" or stay the course when markets get volatile.

I personally am invested entirely in global stocks, because I have a high risk tolerance. My money is invested with a time horizon of decades (as it should be), and I rarely check my returns or worry about how my accounts are doing because I'm well diversified and a committed buy-and-hold investor. This is also how I recommend that you invest.

CLOSING BELL

This may come as a surprise, but investing is the easy part when it comes to building wealth. Don't get me wrong—investing well *really* moves the needle when it comes to accumulating money…but it's not complicated.

The hard part is remembering what you can and can't control and remaining focused only on what you *can* control. You can't control the rate of inflation or what the markets are doing at any point in time. You can control your rate of savings—and your investor behavior.

That liquid net worth figure (see chapter 3) you need to acquire to have total financial independence? For most of us, it's a huge number, and it would be nearly impossible to achieve with saving alone. Investing is the game-changer. You'll be much more likely to get there, and get there faster, with a combination of disciplined saving and investing—especially if you start now.

Another thing you can't control? Taxes. They come for us all. But there *are* things you can do to (legally) keep as much of your money as possible. The next chapter will show you how.

LET'S BREAK IT DOWN

- Investing your money comes with some risk, but so does keeping it in cash.
- Keeping your savings in cash over long periods of time produces the absolute loss of purchasing power due to the eroding effects of inflation and taxes.
- For most millennials, the best and easiest way to cover the costs of taxes and inflation (plus enjoy some true gains) is through a strategy of long-term, buy-and-hold investing into a diversified portfolio of mostly stocks.
- The sooner you put your dollars to "work" in the stock market, the more you'll be able to passively accumulate over the long term through gains generated by a buy-and-hold stock investing strategy.
- Attempts at stock picking and market timing are fools' errands, even for professional investors.
- Millennial investors should have stock portfolios that are widely diversified. Diversification reduces short-term volatility and long-term risk.

CHAPTER 6

THE TAX MAN COMETH

When I first met with my client Talia in 2020, her biggest concern right off the bat was how to lower her tax bill. She was thirty-five and single, and she earned $186,000 a year as an attorney, which put her into the 32 percent federal tax bracket. She had six months of savings in a cash emergency fund and no debts other than a reasonable home mortgage.

Talia had been saving around $35,000 a year into an after-tax savings account, but doing so was a struggle. After inspecting a year-to-date paystub, she was astounded at how much she'd already paid in federal taxes. She felt certain that she could save the same amount or more, while having more money to spend on the "fun stuff," if she could just minimize her tax burden.

I asked Talia if she had a retirement plan offering through work. She thought she did but wasn't sure. So, our next step was a full review of her employee benefits brochure. As it turned out, Talia's employer offered a 401(k) plan and would match her contributions up to 5 percent of her pay. She was also qualified (through her selection of a high-deductible health insurance plan) to contribute to a health savings account (HSA).

I knew that we could easily solve Talia's tax problem while also increasing her savings with two small changes.

First, I advised her to re-route her monthly savings from her savings account to her 401(k) plan by setting up pre-tax payroll deductions into the plan with the goal of hitting the maximum allowable employee contribution each year going forward. Second, I advised her to open and maximally fund a health savings account each year going forward.

The federal government sets maximum funding limits for retirement plans and health savings accounts each year. In 2020 (and 2021), for example, the maximum employee contribution to a 401(k) plan was $19,500 for people under fifty years old. The 2020 maximum individual contribution to an HSA was $3,550 ($3,600 for 2021).

Every pre-tax dollar you contribute to plans like these:

1. Reduces your adjusted gross income (AGI), i.e. your taxable income.
2. Can be invested in stocks and bonds for long-term investment gains.
3. Grows within the account tax-free.

I'll explain these benefits in more detail later in this chapter, but for now, know that taking advantage of these accounts is one of the easiest ways to move the needle when it comes to tax efficiency and wealth building.

Let's break down the savings Talia can expect to see.

By contributing the maximum allowable $19,500 in pre-tax contributions to her 401(k), she knocked that amount right off the top of her taxable income for the year, decreasing her taxable income from $186,000 to $166,500. Her $3,550 HSA contribution further reduced her AGI to $162,950. And just like that, she reduced her taxable income by $23,050 (more than 12 percent) while continuing to save for the future—into accounts that can be invested in stocks to grow and compound tax-free.

Additionally, with the 5 percent contribution match, Talia's employer then kicked another $9,300 into her 401(k)—that's *free* money she was missing out on by not contributing to the plan!

In total:

- Talia's $19,500 in 401(k) contributions
- Plus Talia's $3,550 in HSA contributions
- Plus Talia's employer's $9,300 in 401(k) matching contributions
- Equals $32,350 saved *pre-tax* in investment accounts for Talia's future, only $23,050 of which she actually had to save herself, **and** a 12 percent reduction in taxable income—meaning, she only pays taxes on the lowered amount.

This is one of life's rare "have your cake and eat it too" scenarios.

TAXES: ONE OF LIFE'S FEW CERTAINTIES

What does Talia's example show us? Inefficient tax planning is a major hindrance to wealth building.

And, like Talia, even the most intelligent earners do not have a great understanding of how taxes work. Indeed, tax planning is a massively confusing and complex topic.

From a financial planning perspective, I can boil down a quick and dirty summary of the easiest changes millennial earners can make to (legally) pay less in taxes and free up more cash for saving towards financial independence.

But first, let's look at what exactly taxes are and how they affect you. There are, of course, many types of taxes—but for the purposes of financial planning for the average young accumulator, income taxes are the major focus.

The federal government and many state governments tax your income. This tax is progressive at the federal level (and often at the state level), meaning the more you make, the higher your tax bracket will be. Your filing status—whether you file as single, married filing jointly, married filing separately, or head of household—also affects your tax bracket.

> In most cases, it makes the most financial sense for married people to file jointly because this option usually results in lower taxes. But there are a few exceptions. For example, it may make sense for a married couple to file separately in cases where one spouse has significant itemized deductions that are limited by the couple's combined income, or when doing so would qualify one spouse for a lower income-based student loan repayment.

There are two types of income tax you should understand: taxes on earned income and taxes on unearned income.

TAXES ON EARNED INCOME

Earned-income tax is the tax levied on salaries, wages, bonuses, and tips. There are three main types of taxes on earned income:

- FICA taxes for Social Security and Medicare (aka payroll

taxes): We all pay payroll taxes. In 2021, Social Security tax is 12.4 percent of your wages up to $142,800 (and that upper limit goes up every year) and Medicare tax is 2.9 percent of your income. If you have an employer, they pay half of these payroll taxes on your behalf and the other half is deducted from your paycheck. If you are self-employed, then you have to pay all of it. I recommend looking at a pay stub or W-2 for a better understanding of how this works with your specific information.

- Federal income taxes: The federal government taxes your income. In our opening example, Talia paid payroll taxes as well as federal income taxes in the 32 percent bracket. Here's what that looks like with our current progressive federal tax rates:
    - $0-$9,875 was taxed at 10 percent = $987.50.
    - $9,876-$40,125 was taxed at 12 percent = $3,629.88.
    - $40,126-$85,525 was taxed at 22 percent = $9,987.78.
    - $85,526-$163,300 was taxed at 24 percent = $18,666.76.
    - $163,301-$186,000 was taxed at 32 percent = $7,263.68.
    - For a grand total of $40,175.60 Talia owed in federal taxes. (Note that you don't pay the maximal tax bracket on every dollar you earn but only on the last dollars earned above a given bracket. So every additional dollar earned or deducted applies at your highest bracket. If Talia had earned $190,000, for example, she would be taxed at 32 percent on that additional $4,000.).
    - However, by maxing out her allowable 401(k) and

HSA contributions for the year, Talia reduced her *taxable* income to $162,950, which knocked her down an entire tax bracket to the 24 percent bracket!

- State income taxes: Many states also levy taxes on income, with the brackets and rates varying from state to state.

Add FICA, federal income, and state income taxes together, and you can see that taxes alone can quickly eat up a huge chunk of your income. If you are in a high federal income tax bracket and live in a high-tax state, you may spend over 40 percent of your income on taxes alone!

TAXES ON UNEARNED INCOME

There are also taxes due on unearned income you receive from sources other than working. The main differentiator in the tax treatment of unearned income versus earned income is that unearned income is not subject to payroll taxes (FICA).

For most young people, sources of unearned income might include investment income and real estate income.

- Investment income is just what it sounds like: income you earn on investments—including interest, dividends, and capital gains, all of which are taxed differently.
    - Interest: This includes the returns paid to you from savings and checking accounts, bond investments

(except muni bonds), money you loan to others, and bank CDs. This is taxed at your ordinary income tax rate (meaning, in your income tax bracket).

    - Dividends: Many companies pay dividends to investors who own their stock, distributing some of their profits to stockholders in cash. These dividends are classified as either qualified or unqualified. Qualified dividends are taxed favorably, at a lower rate than ordinary income. Unqualified dividends are taxed at your ordinary income tax rate.
    - Capital gains: This is a tax on the profit you make when you sell an asset for more than you initially paid for it. The rate you are taxed at depends on how long you owned the asset. Assets sold for a gain after less than one year of ownership are deemed to have a short-term capital gain, which is taxed as ordinary income. Assets sold for a gain after more than one year of ownership are deemed to have a long-term capital gain, which is more favorably taxed at rates between 0 percent and 23.8 percent, depending on your income.

- Rental real estate income: If you own rental real estate, this *net* income is taxed as unearned income in your ordinary income bracket (unless you're a professional rental real estate investor, in which case it's taxed as earned income, meaning, you'll also pay payroll taxes).

DEDUCTIONS

As I mentioned earlier, your taxable income is your adjusted gross income, or AGI, which is made up of your earned income plus your unearned income, less any above-the-line deductions you have.

Above-the-line deductions offset your reported income dollar-for-dollar to reduce your AGI. This is important because your AGI is what the IRS uses to determine your eligibility for taking other deductions and credits. The lower your AGI, the more additional deductions and credits you may qualify for. The most widely applicable above-the-line deductions are deductible contributions to retirement plans and deductible contributions to Health Savings Accounts (HSAs).*

*However, some people may qualify for additional above-the-line deductions, including:

- Up to $2,500 in student loan interest (limited by income).
- Qualified tuition expenses.
- Alimony payments established prior to 2019.
- Early withdrawal penalties for savings accounts.
- Health insurance, dental insurance, and long term care insurance premiums for self-employed workers.
- The employer portion of self-employment tax.

Once you arrive at your AGI, you then have two options: 1) take what is called the standard deduction, or 2) itemize deductions.

The standard deduction is a flat amount that everyone is allowed to deduct from their AGI each year, regardless of their income or AGI. For 2021, the standard deduction is $12,550 for single tax filers and $25,100 for people who are married filing jointly.

Your other option is to itemize deductions by deducting certain specific expenses you may have had. These are typically referred to as below-the-line deductions. These include medical expenses over a certain percentage of your AGI, property taxes, state and local taxes, and mortgage interest on mortgages up to $750,000, among others, and they are subject to limitations, floors, and ceilings.

You cannot both take the standard deduction and itemize deductions; you must choose one or the other. To determine whether you should take the standard deduction or itemize deductions, just compare your Schedule A, or itemized deductions, to your standard deduction amount and take whichever is larger.

Let's take a simple example:

Ashley is a single filer. For 2020, she had a gross income of

$170,000 and made $12,000 in deductible contributions to her 401(k). She had no other above-the-line deductions for 2020. Her AGI is $158,000:

$170,000 gross income - $12,000 above-the-line deductions = $158,000 AGI

Her possible below-the-line deductions total $10,500. She will come out ahead by taking the 2020 standard deduction of $12,400 for single filers rather than taking her $10,500 in itemized deductions. The $12,400 standard deduction is then taken from her AGI, to arrive at a taxable income of $145,600.

> Another term you should understand is your modified adjusted gross income, or MAGI. Your MAGI determines whether you're eligible for certain tax credits and whether you can contribute to a traditional deductible IRA or a Roth IRA. It's usually higher than your AGI because its calculation adds back in certain deductions that are removed from gross income to get to your AGI.

HOW TAXES AFFECT YOU—AND HOW YOU CAN AFFECT YOUR TAXES

You should be taking steps proactively, throughout each calendar year, to maximize tax savings.

There are tons of complex strategies for lowering your tax bill, and an entire industry dedicated to doing just that. But for the average millennial saver, it is not that complicated. I recommend that you focus on just two *major*—yet simple—strategies for building wealth in a tax-efficient manner:

1. Maximize contributions to tax-preferred retirement accounts.
2. Earn money on investments that are taxed as long-term capital gains.

I have a friend who makes $250,000 a year and spends nearly everything she takes home. She's not maxing out her 401(k), and yet she complains incessantly about how her tax burden has grown along with her income. She called me last April a few days shy of the prior year filing deadline wondering if I had some magical, painless strategy for reducing her tax bill. I told her the same thing I'm telling you: the easiest way for just about anybody to save money on taxes is by contributing to a pre-tax retirement plan. (She actually responded, "Oh. I thought it would be something more fun." Ha!)

INCREASING TAX EFFICIENCY WITH RETIREMENT PLAN CONTRIBUTIONS

Once you are in a position to start saving discretionary income, you have a lot of options. If you are like many other young accumulators (not yet at peak earnings), then you may not be able to maximally fund all of your goals at once. As I noted in the last chapter, you should revisit chapter 3 if you have questions about how to prioritize your cash flows between emergency fund accrual, debt reduction, near-term purchase goals, and investing.

Once you're in the financial position to do so (and if you're not, it should be your goal to get there ASAP), there are some very compelling reasons why maximally funding tax-preferred retirement accounts should be your top savings strategy.

First, retirement plan funding can be one of the easiest ways to automate paying yourself first (which is one of the top cash flow planning strategies I recommend, as you'll remember from chapter 3). This is especially true for workers with access to an employer-sponsored plan such as a 401(k) or 403(b). In this case, funding usually means a one-time set up of payroll deductions that will continue going forward with no action needed from you.

Second, funding tax-preferred retirement plans is (for most earners) the most efficient way to save a lot of money. What do I mean by efficient? Think of it this way: for every dollar you earn in the 35 percent tax bracket, you have to earn $1.35 just to save one dollar of after-tax money (and that's just federal taxes—not including payroll or state taxes!). However, if you want to save a dollar into a pre-tax retirement account such as an IRA or a 401k, you only have to earn a dollar, regardless of what tax bracket you're in! It is easier to save a dollar before tax than after tax.

Third, many employer-sponsored plans offer some sort of free money incentive for employees who contribute, most often in the form of a match or profit sharing. Need I say more? This actually is free money that your employer is putting towards *your* future! This alone should be incentive to contribute at least enough to get the full match if your employer offers one.

Fourth, one of the biggest incentives of all is tax-free compounding of gains. When you invest your contributions within a tax-preferred retirement account, your invested money and the gains that compound over time can grow tax-free for decades. If you invest wisely, as I've described in chapter 5, down the road you will end up with *much* more than you contributed.

Finally, another advantage for most people using a tax-preferred retirement plan is the difference in tax rates when they are in their earning years versus their retirement years. The vast majority of us are in a higher tax bracket while earning and trying to save than when we are taking money out of the retirement plan after work stops. Essentially, the government has "loaned" you the money you would have paid in taxes to grow tax-deferred, and you will then pay it back in a lower tax bracket.

Let me explain that by revisiting an example from chapter 5:

If you invested $20,000 into an S&P 500 fund on January 1, 1990, within a (non-retirement) after-tax brokerage account and never touched it again, it would have been worth $195,000 on January 1, 2020. If you then sold it all on January 1, 2020, you would be taxed on the long-term capital gain, leaving you with *net* proceeds of $168,750, assuming a 15 percent capital gains bracket.

If instead, that same scenario occurred within a tax-preferred retirement account, there would be *no tax at all* due upon the sale of the investment—regardless of how large the gain is. You would have the entire $195,000 to reinvest within the account.

Now, you will pay income tax on money withdrawn down the road (the government will force you to start taking money out eventually, currently starting at age seventy-two). However, the overwhelming majority of people will be in a lower bracket when they start taking withdrawals than they were in their prime earning years (presumably when they were making deductible contributions). Thus, in the majority of cases, this is a great deal.

There are multiple kinds of retirement plans, most of which are employer-provided—and all of which come with some kind of preferential tax treatment. The main differentiator between types of tax-preferred retirement plans is whether you make contributions with pre-tax or post-tax dollars.

Traditionally, most retirement accounts are funded with

pre-tax contributions. Logistically, this means that contributions are either taken from your paycheck by your employer before the rest is delivered to you, or you contribute with after-tax dollars and then deduct that amount at tax time. Either way, the amount you contribute is removed from your taxable income.

You also have the option of making after-tax contributions to some plans. This is often referred to as making Roth contributions, as in the case of a Roth IRA, or in employer-sponsored retirement plans that allow for this.

Of course, the government *will* take its share eventually, one way or another. And while there are great efficiencies to be found by taking advantage of tax-preferred accounts, it's important that you understand that *tax-preferred does not mean tax-free*.

You'll always pay taxes at some point, whether you do so upon putting money into an investment or upon taking it out. The only exception to this is funding an HSA, which we'll talk about later in this chapter.

For now, let's take a closer look at pre- and post-tax retirement accounts.

PAYING TAXES ON THE TAIL END WITH PRE-TAX RETIREMENT PLANS

Most people have at least one option for saving money in a pre-tax fashion. Pre-tax savings opportunities include most employer-sponsored retirement plans (401(k), 403(b), SEP-IRA, SIMPLE IRA) and traditional IRAs.

Note: "employer-provided" does not mean that self-employed workers are excluded from funding these plans. If you are self-employed, *you* are the employer.

401(k) and 403(b)

Two very common employer-provided plans are 401(k)s and 403(b)s, which are essentially the same as 401(k)s but are most commonly offered to teachers and healthcare workers.

These plans often have a "free money" component in that they frequently include some employer contribution into employee accounts, either in the form of a contribution match or in what is called employer profit sharing.

Money that *you* contribute to the plan (and the earnings on it) is always yours, and can be moved by you if you separate from employment. Money that your employer contributes on your behalf sometimes vests (i.e. becomes fully yours to own) on a schedule. For example, a common vesting schedule is: 20 percent of employer contributions into your account will vest after two years of service, 40 percent after three years of service, 60 percent after four years of service, 80 percent after five years of service, and 100 percent after six years of service. The time period when your employer's contributions become fully yours varies from plan to plan.

For 2020 and 2021, a person under age fifty can put $19,500 in pre-tax dollars towards employee salary deferral contributions, which reduce your taxable income dollar for dollar.

Traditional Pre-Tax IRA

Traditional pre-tax individual retirement accounts (IRAs) are not employer sponsored. They are very simple to open and fund, but your ability to make deductible contributions is subject to a relatively low income ceiling if you (or your spouse) are covered by an employer-sponsored retirement plan. These income limitations change every year, so you can look them up if you're interested.

People under fifty who are eligible to make deductible contributions can contribute up to $6,000 pre-tax to a Traditional IRA for 2020 and 2021.

SEP IRAs

A Simplified Employee Pension Individual Retirement Account, or SEP IRA, is a good option for self-employed workers and small business owners with few or no employees. Just like with a traditional IRA, your pre-tax contributions grow tax-free within the account and are subject to essentially the same withdrawal rules.

Only employers make contributions to these plans. Employers can contribute up to 25 percent of W-2 income or up to $58,000 (whichever is lower) in pre-tax dollars for 2021.

SIMPLE IRAs

Savings Incentive Match Plan for Employees Individual Retirement Accounts, or SIMPLE IRAs, are employer-sponsored retirement plans mostly for small businesses. As with the other accounts we have looked at, contributions are pre-tax and grow tax-free.

Employees under the age of fifty can contribute up to $13,500 for 2020 and 2021. Employers are either required to match employee contributions up to 3 percent of their pay (after two years) or make a non-elective 2 percent of pay contribution for every employee.

If you are not covered by an employer-sponsored retirement plan—either because your employer does not offer one, or you're self-employed—you still have plenty of options!

If you're self-employed or have any 1099 income from a side hustle, you can open a Self-Employed 401(k), a SIMPLE IRA, a SEP IRA, or a Traditional IRA to shelter some self-employment income from taxes and save for the future. After all, you are the employer (and employee).

Self Employed 401(k) plans are usually the best option for the most aggressive savers because of the relatively high contribution limits. In 2021, for example, a self-employed worker could use a Solo or Self Employed 401(k) to put away, pre-tax, up to $19,500 in "employee" contributions, plus up to (roughly) 20 percent of net income in deductible "employer" contributions, with an upper limit of $57,000 in total contributions. If you have the cash flow to fund this and invest well, you can easily accumulate a seven-figure account in record time.

If you're not self-employed, have no source of 1099 income, and are not covered by an employer-sponsored plan, you may still be able to contribute earned income to a Traditional or Roth IRA, depending on your income, tax filing status, and whether your spouse is covered by an employer-sponsored plan. And finally, if you're not eligible for an employer-sponsored plan and cannot make deductible IRA or Roth IRA contributions, you may be eligible to do a backdoor Roth IRA conversion—see below for more on that.

Bottom line: most people have *some* option for tax-preferred saving, and it's not difficult to get started. You can open and fund these accounts at almost any large financial institution.

Withdrawing Money from Pre-Tax Plans

The government is giving you a big break by allowing you to save into these plans pre-tax. They hope that you'll use the accounts to save and invest responsibly, to accumulate a large enough nest egg that will provide for your future self during retirement.

This is why there is a 10 percent penalty for withdrawing pre-tax funds from these plans before the age of fifty-nine-and-a-half. Withdrawals taken after age fifty-nine-and-a-half are taxed as ordinary income, but there is no penalty. Once you hit seventy-two (under current laws), the government actually forces you to take some money out each year. As with early withdrawals, funds withdrawn at this point will be taxed as ordinary income. By that time, you'll presumably be retired and in a lower tax bracket than you were while you were working and funding the account.

One of the biggest financial mistakes I see young earners make is viewing the funds in their retirement accounts as another "pot" of potential spending money and taking withdrawals prior to retirement.

In the worst cases, I see young professionals withdrawing retirement plan funds for the purchase of depreciating assets (like cars) or consumption items. An earner in a 35 percent tax bracket who takes a withdrawal from a 401(k) to pay for a car will lose at least 45 percent of the withdrawn funds to taxes and the penalty, only to then put the remaining funds into an asset that is guaranteed to lose value rapidly.

> That is bad financial behavior at its worst—a pattern that destroys wealth and should be avoided at all costs.

I also see young people withdraw funds unintentionally, without realizing that they are doing so, typically when they separate from an employer. If you separate from employment and have funds in an employer-sponsored retirement plan, you typically have the option to *roll* the plan (tax-free) into another pre-tax retirement plan, such as an IRA or another employer's plan, as opposed to withdrawing the plan assets. It is a mistake to withdraw the funds!

A NOTE ON HSA PLANS

Health savings accounts, or HSAs, are technically not retirement plans, but you can think of them like IRAs for healthcare expenses. Not everyone has access to one of these plans, but you may be eligible to fund an HSA if you are covered by a qualifying high deductible health insurance plan (known as a HDHP). Maximum funding limits for 2021 are $3,600 for individuals and $7,200 for families.

Most importantly, HSA funds are *triple tax-free* if used for healthcare expenses:

1. Funds you contribute are tax deductible.
2. They can be invested within the account for tax-free growth.
3. And, unlike with any pre-tax retirement plan, funds can be withdrawn tax-free if used for healthcare expenses.

This is literally the *only* legal way to completely avoid paying taxes.

If you have the cash flow to fund one of these accounts and are eligible to do so, I highly recommend it. Funds you don't use for current healthcare expenses can sit in the account to grow for decades just as with any other retirement plan.

PAYING TAXES ON THE FRONT END WITH AFTER-TAX RETIREMENT ACCOUNT CONTRIBUTIONS

If you are in a relatively low tax bracket now, it may make more sense to fund a retirement account with after-tax retirement contributions rather than pre-tax.

The most popular way for young accumulators to do this is by contributing to a Roth IRA.

Roth IRAs

A Roth IRA is an individual (not employer-sponsored) retirement account that you can fund with after-tax dollars (i.e., dollars sitting in your checking account). Note, however, that the ability to contribute to a Roth IRA is subject to strict income phase-outs. For 2021, the phase-out starts at $125,000 MAGI for singles and $198,000 MAGI for married filers.

If eligible, you can make a full Roth IRA contribution ($6,000 for 2021) while also contributing to a pre-tax employer-sponsored plan like a 401(k), SEP IRA, or SIMPLE IRA. You cannot, however, contribute more than $6,000 total between a traditional pre-tax IRA and a Roth IRA in any year, so it is best to pick one or the other.

Funds you contribute to a Roth IRA are not deductible but do grow tax-free within the account, as with pre-tax retirement plans. However, after age fifty-nine-and-a-half, all funds in a Roth IRA, including investment earnings, can be withdrawn completely tax- and penalty-free!

You can always withdraw your contributions (not earnings) tax-free, regardless of your age. The government cares less about regulating your use of your own after-tax contributions to these accounts because they already taxed you on the front end.

Roth vs. Pre-Tax Retirement Accounts

If you're eligible to make Roth IRA or after-tax Roth retirement plan contributions, how do you choose between the two?

The answer primarily comes down to your tax bracket. If you think that your tax bracket now is relatively low compared with what it might be down the road—in other words, that your peak earning years are ahead of you—then it makes sense to "make hay while the sun shines" and pay taxes in your currently low bracket rather than down the road. This is especially true in the case of a Roth IRA—if your income qualifies you to contribute to a Roth IRA, it likely makes sense for you to contribute.*

*The same logic applies for Roth or after-tax contributions to a 401(k) or 403(b).

Generally, the higher your tax bracket, the more it makes sense for you to prioritize pre-tax savings over after-tax savings, because it becomes more and more likely that your tax bracket will be lower when you take withdrawals than it is while you're contributing.

BACKDOOR ROTH IRA CONTRIBUTIONS FOR HIGHER EARNERS

High earners are disqualified from contributing to Roth IRAs, but there is a loophole called a backdoor Roth IRA conversion that anyone can use regardless of tax bracket.

Mechanically, this is a process by which you funnel after-tax money through a traditional IRA account into a Roth IRA. Once the funds are in the Roth IRA, they can grow and contributions can be withdrawn tax-free (after an initial five-year period). Note that using a backdoor Roth process is not advantageous from a tax perspective if you have any pre-tax IRA money floating around. This really only makes sense for high earners with no pre-tax IRA money who have already maximized all available pre-tax savings options. If you are in this scenario, doing backdoor Roth conversions each year is a great way to build up a nest egg of non-taxable retirement savings.

HOW AND WHEN TO FUND YOUR RETIREMENT ACCOUNT

It can be hard to decide what to do when you have a finite amount of money to save and multiple options for where to save it. How do you know when to start funneling your savings into a retirement account? And how much should you invest?

First, revisit the cash flow planning and debt chapters (chapters 3 and 4) and take another look at my debt versus investing matrix (in chapter 3). If you have at least six months of expenses set aside in an emergency fund and no urgent debt to pay down, then you are likely a good candidate for funding a retirement plan.

If you are also saving for an after-tax goal, like a down payment fund, I don't recommend that you prioritize that over retirement savings for very long. Ideally, you'll be able to save for your after-tax goal while also at least funding your retirement plan to some degree.

If you have a high income, you should make it your goal to:

- Maximize pre-tax retirement contributions.
- Contribute the maximum to an HSA if possible.
- Do annual backdoor Roth IRA conversions (if you have no pre-tax IRA money).
- Invest extra cash into an after-tax (non-retirement) brokerage account.

If you are not yet at a place where you can max out retirement plan contributions, don't be discouraged! You can still do quite well if you start saving now. If a thirty-year-old starts putting just $10,000 into his 401(k) every year with a 7 percent investment return, he will have $300,000 in contributions by age sixty. His earnings on those contributions, however, will provide him with a total account value of $1.086 million!

It's okay if you're not ready to max out. Start with what you can do, and increase your contribution amount each year until you are at the max. Even just increasing your contributions by 1 percent each year makes a difference, and you surely won't notice that extra 1 percent. And, throwing it back to chapter 3, this is a great way to save half of every raise. If you're not maxing out, allocate half of every raise to increasing retirement plan contributions until you are.

FURTHER REDUCE YOUR TAX BURDEN THROUGH LONG-TERM CAPITAL GAINS

Now that we've covered the ins and outs of reducing taxes by maximizing savings into tax-preferred retirement plans, we'll cover the other major way to build wealth in a tax-efficient manner: accumulating money that is favorably taxed as long-term capital gains.

We've established that one of the primary benefits of retirement accounts is the tax-preferred growth of assets within the account. You can sell an investment within a retirement account for a massive profit and pay no tax at all until the money is withdrawn, even if this is many years later (or, in the case of Roth accounts, pay no tax on realized profits ever again).

Outside of retirement accounts, however, a profit resulting from selling an asset for more than you initially paid is taxed as a capital gain. Recall from earlier in the chapter that assets sold for a gain after less than one year of ownership are deemed to have a short-term capital gain (STCG), and are taxed as ordinary income. Assets sold for a gain after more than one year of ownership are deemed to have a long-term capital gain (LTCG). LTCG tax rates are favorable as compared with ordinary income tax rates, with LTCGs being taxed at rates between 0 percent and 23.8 percent*, depending on your income. Remember that the highest tax bracket for ordinary earned income is currently 37 percent.

*Including a 3.8 percent Medicare surtax on net investment income for high earners.

For that reason, after funding tax-preferred retirement vehicles, accumulating money that will be taxed as LTCG is one of the most tax-efficient ways to amass further wealth.

For most millennials, the simplest way to do this is through long-term, buy-and-hold stock investing, as described in chapter 5, in an individual or joint after-tax investment account (a simple brokerage account, as opposed to a tax-preferred retirement account as described above). If you fully fund all tax-preferred investment accounts available to you and still have extra cash for long-term investing, this is what you should be doing with it.

Let's again take Talia's example from earlier in the chapter. Recall that Talia was able to greatly increase her tax efficiency by maximizing contributions to the pre-tax retirement vehicles that were available to her. Talia's next best option for further investing is after-tax investing—meaning, she can invest the leftover cash that is now sitting in her bank account after payroll and income taxes were deducted.

Let's say Talia regularly uses her extra cash to invest $10,000 a year into an after-tax brokerage account over the next decade. Because she is a disciplined buy-and-hold investor, she invests into a mix of widely diversified stock funds and lets them sit and grow over the years. After ten years, her $100,000 in contributions to her after-tax stock portfolio has grown to $157,000 due to the compounding of gains on the stock funds over that period.

So far, none of this $57,000 gain has been taxed at all—and it won't be taxed as long as she doesn't sell the stocks. Capital gains are only taxed when *realized*, aka when you *sell* an asset for a profit. The value of Talia's stock portfolio could continue to grow tremendously over the decades, and she will never pay tax on the gains within the account until she sells the underlying assets (stock funds). Even then, the gains will be taxed at LTCG rates of 0 percent to 23.8 percent (depending on her income at that time), as opposed to higher ordinary income tax rates.

> Note that some profits from sales of real estate are also taxed as capital gains, but if the sale is of your primary home, you can exclude up to $250,000 of gain as a single filer, or $500,000 of gain as married filers, from taxation.

The good news is that you can benefit from this strategy, too! Many of my older clients have doubled or tripled their wealth (or more) simply by investing in this way over the years. Billionaire or not, this is one of the most surefire ways to passively build wealth for just about anyone.

Remember that short-term capital gains—those resulting from the sale of assets held for less than a year—are taxed as ordinary income, so usually at much higher rates. I highly discourage short-term trading and investing for several reasons, and this is a big one.

SIMPLE, STRAIGHTFORWARD STRATEGIES

Taxes can be a real drain on your resources, and tax planning can be very intimidating, even for sophisticated professionals. For the ultra-wealthy, complex tax planning is warranted. But the majority of people—especially you, reading this book—

will come out *far* ahead just by implementing the two simple but powerful tax strategies we discussed in this chapter:

1. Maximize contributions to tax-preferred retirement accounts.
2. Earn money on investments that are taxed as long-term capital gains.

If you do just these two things, and you invest wisely (as discussed in chapter 5), you can become wealthy.

That's it. Sorry there's no magic wand!

LET'S BREAK IT DOWN

- Inefficient tax planning is a major hindrance to building wealth.
- We all have to pay taxes. These taxes may be on earned income (in the form of federal, state, and FICA taxes for Social Security and Medicare—aka payroll taxes) or on unearned income (income from investments or real estate, for example).
- For the average millennial saver, the two most powerful strategies for building wealth in a more tax-efficient manner are:

1. Maximizing contributions to tax-preferred retirement accounts (whether through pre-tax plans, such as 401(k), 403(b), SEP-IRA, SIMPLE IRA, and traditional IRAs; or after-tax plans, such as Roth IRAs).
2. Accumulating money that is taxed at the relatively favorable long-term capital gains rate.

CHAPTER 7

CREATING YOUR OWN SAFETY NET

Ben was a young, thriving small business owner when he ran a red light and T-boned another vehicle on the way to work one day. Unfortunately, both he and the driver of the other car were seriously injured in the collision, and both required hospitalization and multiple surgeries.

The other driver sued Ben and obtained a judgment of $1.2 million against him for the injuries the driver suffered as a result of the collision.

Ben's auto policy, which included the standard $500,000 in personal liability coverage, wrote the other driver a check for $500,000 and closed out the claim, leaving Ben on the hook for the remaining $700,000. The court seized Ben's

$200,000 after-tax nest egg to go towards the balance of the judgment, but after that, there was nothing left to take. Ben still owed $500,000 and had no idea where he would get it.

As if that wasn't bad enough, Ben's business had floundered in his prolonged absence after the accident, and he wasn't able to work consistently going forward due to ongoing mobility and cognitive issues, so his income had all but disappeared.

"How did I end up here?" Ben wondered. He'd worked hard his entire life to be responsible and financially independent. He'd built a successful business, worked hard, lived within his means, and accumulated a decent nest egg. Now it felt like all of that had been erased in the blink of an eye. Where did he go wrong?

KEEPING YOUR F-YOU MONEY

That story may sound like a fear mongering insurance ad to you, but I assure you, it's a real-life scenario that is completely plausible—and more common than you would think.

Sooner or later, sh*t happens to most of us. But you can weave a strong safety net for yourself, using a variety of tools and strategies I'll discuss in this chapter, to better protect your family, your assets, and your wellbeing from many of the hardships that life might throw at you.

So far, we've discussed strategies for *building* wealth, including strategic cash flow planning, paying off debt, and investing in a tax-efficient manner. But a complete financial plan also includes strategies for *protecting* that accumulated wealth.

Like everything else in this book, there is no cookie-cutter answer for exactly what tools *you* should use to construct *your* safety net. This is a high-level overview of what most young people should consider, and I recommend that you tailor your implementation of this advice to fit your own specific circumstances.

I've broken this chapter into two main sections: the first is on protecting your assets, and the second is on protecting yourself and your family.

A WORD ON INSURANCE

Heads up—we're going to be talking about insurance in this chapter, and when most people (myself included) hear the word "insurance," they think, "Oh no, someone is about to try to sell me something."

The insurance industry certainly has some (okay, many) bad actors and scam artists, and they've given the whole industry a bad name.

But in all likelihood, you do need some insurance—almost everyone does. If you're a millennial professional, you likely need *at least* liability insurance and disability insurance in addition to standard insurance like auto and health.

Insurance is an incredibly powerful tool for risk management and asset protection, and is often the one thing preventing a life catastrophe from also becoming a financial catastrophe. To use the cliché, it's something you need but hope to never use. When you do need to use it, boy, are you glad to have it.

PROTECT YOUR ASS...ETS

Asset protection becomes increasingly important once you start to accumulate significant assets, but it's also important while you're early in the accumulation stage. Ben's story is a great illustration of this.

When you are young, two of the worst things that can happen to you financially are for you to lose your ability to earn an income, or to have a significant monetary judgment entered against you. Unless you are already quite wealthy, financial setbacks like these can be very hard to recover from.

It is my job to anticipate the possibility of scenarios like Ben's and make sure that my clients are well set up and protected from any potential financial ramifications of unexpected life derailments like these. My dad likes to say that each individual asset protection measure you put in place is like a fence around your assets. While any one individual fence might not completely prevent a loss of assets, each additional "fence" adds another barrier, another layer of protection.

I like to think of asset protection measures more like ropes in your safety net—one rope alone is helpful, but it only goes so far. But a combination of measures or "ropes" woven together lowers the chances of you falling through the cracks.

Whether you think of them as fences or ropes, some of the most effective asset protection measures that most people should consider are: umbrella liability insurance, uninsured motorist insurance, and proper car titling.

I'll discuss each in turn.

> Note: I will only discuss asset protection measures here that are appropriate for consideration by most of my potential readers. There are, of course, many other, and more "niche-y," asset protection tools and strategies that are less widely applicable but are highly advantageous for certain people. For example, business owners should seek out specialized advice on business liability insurance and the potential use of protective entities like LLCs for asset protection.

UMBRELLA LIABILITY INSURANCE

Nearly everyone should have a personal liability umbrella policy with coverage of at least $2 million. If you are found to be personally liable for causing harm to another person, this policy will (very likely) cover you.

In the case of an auto liability judgment, for example, an umbrella policy "steps in" and pays for damages you owe beyond what your auto policy will cover, up to the limit of the umbrella policy.

Let's go back to the Ben example. If Ben had a $2 million umbrella policy, here's how things would have gone:

- His auto insurer would have paid $500,000 of the $1.2 million judgment, per his liability coverage of $500,000 on the auto policy.
- Then, his umbrella insurer would have paid the $700,000 balance of the judgment.
- The other driver would have been paid all he was owed, and the court wouldn't have seized Ben's life savings.

In this scenario, both Ben and the other injured driver are much better off financially.

If you are like most people, a car accident is probably your number-one source of potential liability, so having umbrella liability coverage goes a long way towards protecting your assets. Think of it like putting a couple million bucks between your assets and a potential creditor. But umbrella policies don't just cover you for auto liability. In fact, they are called "umbrella" policies because the scope of their coverage is quite broad. Among other things, an umbrella policy will, for example, cover you for liability that arises from someone being injured while on your property.

Importantly, these policies are incredibly cheap and very easy to obtain. You should be able to get coverage with one or two phone calls to your auto or homeowner's/renter's insurer, and you shouldn't pay more than $300 to $400 per year, per million dollars in coverage. No excuses!

> People with more exposure to risk should get more umbrella coverage. If, for example, you:
>
> - Own a dangerous toy like a trampoline or a jet ski.
> - Own a rental unit.
> - Have anyone else (such as a nanny) driving around town in a car that's titled in your name.
>
> Then you need all the umbrella liability insurance you can get!

UNINSURED MOTORIST COVERAGE:

You may or may not have some uninsured/underinsured motorist coverage (UIM) on your auto policy, but you could probably benefit from having more.

If you and/or your vehicle are harmed in a collision with a driver who is uninsured, or underinsured, your uninsured motorist coverage will cover your costs, up to the limit of the policy. This is one that tends to fly under the radar, but I've seen enough to know that having this coverage is an essential part of your safety net, and it's worth every penny. It's exactly the kind of policy you don't know you need until it's too late.

There are a ton of uninsured motorists driving around. If you don't have UIM coverage, you'll be out-of-luck if one of them causes you grievous bodily harm or property damage.

Most uninsured motorist policies have coverage of $300,000/$500,000. I recommend that you have at least $1 million in UIM coverage. Depending on your insurer, you should be able to get this level of coverage either on your underlying auto policy or by adding uninsured motorist coverage to your umbrella policy. As with the umbrella, adding this is as simple as making a phone call.

CAR TITLING

Correctly titling your car, in addition to having personal liability umbrella insurance and UIM coverage, is one of the easiest ways to reduce your liability exposure, and it's very simple.

You, and every person in your family, should be driving cars that are titled *solely* in the name of the primary driver.

Here's why: if your spouse causes an accident while driving a car that is titled in your name, the resulting plaintiff/creditor could sue you as the car's owner *and* your spouse as the car's driver. The same scenario would ensue in the case of a jointly titled car. When both you and your spouse are sued, your individual assets, your spouse's individual assets, and your joint assets are all potentially up for grabs in the case of a large monetary judgment.

If, instead, your spouse causes an accident while driving a car titled solely in their name, only they can be named in a resulting lawsuit, and only their assets would be on the table to satisfy a large judgment.

Modern day car accident judgments can cost millions of dollars. Having umbrella liability coverage is your first line of defense for auto liability, but having your cars properly titled is another easy asset protection "rope" to add to your safety net, at little to no cost.

ASSETS WITH INHERENT PROTECTION

Now for some good news: some assets are inherently protected from creditors by federal and/or state laws.

ERISA retirement plans such as 401(k)s and most 403(b)s are well protected from most creditors by federal law. IRA assets of up to $1 million are also protected by federal law, and many state laws have an even higher degree of protection for IRA assets. Bottom line, it's unlikely that a creditor could take your retirement plan assets. Most after-tax assets, such as non-retirement investment accounts and bank accounts, do not have inherent asset protection.

> Many states also protect the equity in your home from creditors. In Florida, for example, 100 percent of the equity in your primary home is protected from creditors. Other states have more limited protection, but some is better than nothing!

In Ben's case from the beginning of this chapter, his $200,000 nest egg would have been insulated from garnishment had it been contained in a retirement plan. This inherent asset protection feature is just one more reason to maximally fund these plans.

PROTECTING YOURSELF AND YOUR FAMILY

This section relies upon one tool with many pieces, like a Swiss army knife, to protect you and your family (if you have one) in case something bad happens to you. That tool is insurance.

The three types of insurance I'll discuss here are health insurance, disability insurance, and life insurance.

HEALTH INSURANCE

I'm not going to go too deep on health insurance because it's subject to the whims of politicians—and it's more complicated than it should be.

I would like to think that I don't even need to say that we all need health insurance, but I know a few people running around without it. So here goes: *everyone absolutely needs health insurance*.

Okay, with that established, it's also good to have a basic knowledge of how health insurance works and understand a few of the key terms used to distinguish one plan from another.

Whether you have health insurance options through an employer or get individual coverage through the marketplace, your choice will come down to a trade-off between the level of coverage you have and the premiums you pay for it. In most cases, paying higher premiums means you'll have lower deductibles, co-pays, and coinsurance (and vice versa).

- A deductible is the amount of money you have to pay towards your own healthcare in a year before your health insurance kicks in to start covering the cost. Deductible levels commonly vary between $1,000 and $7,000.
- When you're looking at insurance options, coinsurance is typically listed as a percentage for various services. For

example, a hospital stay may have 20 percent coinsurance, which means that you will pay 20 percent of the cost and your insurance will cover the other 80 percent.

- Co-pays are typically listed as a flat amount you'll pay to a medical provider for services. For example, a $50 co-pay for any specialist visit.

> For any service with a co-pay or coinsurance listed, you will pay that amount until you hit your maximum out-of-pocket.

The last big term you should know with regards to health insurance is your out-of-pocket maximum. This is another number you'll usually see listed along with the deductible. The out-of-pocket maximum is just what it sounds like: the most you will have to pay overall towards covered healthcare in a year, period.

Let's say, for example, that you have a policy with a $4,000 deductible and an out-of-pocket maximum of $8,000. That means that if you need medical care, you have to spend $4,000 of your own money (in addition to the premiums you pay for coverage) before your insurance kicks in. Once they start paying, they will do it in such a way that you are still also paying some part of your healthcare costs (co-pays and coinsurance) until you have paid a total of $8,000 for the benefit period. The insurer pays for all covered services after you hit your out-of-pocket maximum.

However—and this is a big however—both deductibles and maximum out-of-pockets tend to apply separately for in-network care and out-of-network care. For example, a typical policy might have limits of:

- $3,000 deductible/$7,000 out-of-pocket maximum for in-network care.
- $7,000 deductible/$15,000 out-of-pocket maximum for out-of-network care.

Insurers have "networks" of care providers with whom they have contractual agreements. Coverage tends to be much better for you if you stay "in-network" for care, as the deductibles and out-of-pockets are lower. But this isn't always possible. Sometimes, especially during an emergency, you can't avoid receiving out-of-network care, and this will likely mean large medical bills for you.

It's important to know your maximum out of pocket figures for both in-network and out-of-network care, because that number likely represents the worst-case scenario for you. No matter what happens, whether you have $9,000 of medical expenses in a year or $30,000, you will pay a maximum of $7,000 for covered in-network care and $15,000 for covered out-of-network care, if those are the out-of-pocket maximums for your policy. Charges for in-network care do not accrue progress towards your deductible or out-of-pocket maximum for out-of-network care, and vice-versa.

Sometimes it's hard to decide where you should put your money in this expensive endeavor of protecting your physical body. Should you pay more monthly so you can pay less if something big happens? Or should you pay less each month with the expectation of having a higher bill in case of an unforeseen medical emergency.

My answer, of course, is "it depends."

If you know that you are going to have high medical expenses, it's probably worth paying higher premiums for a policy with a lower deductible—sometimes described as platinum policies. But if you're super healthy and don't anticipate needing high cost medical care, you might opt for a policy with a higher deducible and lower monthly premium.

Policies on the higher end of the deductible spectrum are frequently referred to as high-deductible health plans or HDHPs. Participating in a plan that is designated as a HDHP qualifies you to fund an HSA, which we know from the last chapter is the only legal way to completely avoid paying taxes! If you do participate in a HDHP, I *highly* recommend that you fund a health savings account so that you have the option of paying for healthcare expenses with pre-tax dollars, which does take the sting out of the higher deductible.

I know—what a mess. It makes even my head hurt. As

I'm sure you're aware, healthcare is always up for legislative debate and all of this may change by the time I publish this book. But for now, that's the state of health insurance, and you'll be better off if you know the basics.

DISABILITY INSURANCE

The next essential component of any safety net is disability insurance coverage.

Becoming disabled is catastrophic enough to begin with, but it is also one of the most financially catastrophic things that can happen to you because being disabled can be very expensive, while in many cases simultaneously taking away your ability to earn an income.

If you think you're not at risk for becoming disabled, think again. All of us are at constant risk of possibly becoming disabled just by being out in the world. Life can change in the blink of an eye, and anyone who has fallen victim to an unexpected disabling event knows this all too well. Although we can't totally eliminate the risk of becoming disabled, we can at least insure against the financial consequences that come with disability.

How do you know if you need disability insurance? Well, just answer one simple question: If you became disabled tomorrow in a way that took away your ability to earn an income for the rest of your life, would you or your loved ones suffer financially?

If the answer is yes—and it is for most people—then you need disability insurance. This is especially true for millennials. Being nearer to the start of their careers than the end, a loss of income due to disability would cause significant financial stress to even high-earning, well-off millennial workers who don't have insurance to replace lost income.

There are two types of disability insurance: short-term coverage and long-term coverage. Within both short- and long-term disability, there are different levels of coverage as well, including own-occupation policies and non-own-occupation policies.

Non-own occupation policies, to varying degrees, tend not to distinguish between whether you can work at all, versus whether you can perform the duties of your specific job or specialty. An extreme example of this would be, "Sorry you can't practice neurosurgery anymore, but if you can push a broom, you can work."

Own-occupation policies, on the other hand, are specifically written to qualify you for benefits if your disabling event is a hindrance to you performing the duties of your *specific* job. Though more expensive, I recommend that everybody get own-occupation coverage, for obvious reasons.

Short-term disability insurance is what it sounds like: insurance coverage for short-term disability events, typically those lasting for ninety days or fewer that result in a loss of income. After an unpaid waiting period (called an elimination period) starting from the day your disability is certified by a doctor, these policies pay you benefits that replace some portion of your lost income—typically around 60 percent—if you go on disability.

With most good policies, it's possible to claim disability for any condition that interferes with your ability to do your job, so it varies depending on what your job is. If your job is very physical, a back injury that makes work impossible for two months would likely qualify you for benefits. As another example, many women with short-term disability coverage are able to receive short-term disability benefits after delivering a baby and taking unpaid maternity leave.

On the other hand, I have the example of a client of mine who's a radiologist. Much of his job is sitting in a room, reading scans all day. When I encouraged him to get disability insurance, he laughed and said, "Do you know how hard it is to qualify for benefits as a radiologist? I could lose a limb, I could go deaf, hell I could lose one of my eyes, and I could still read scans."

So, again, it really depends on your specific job and to what degree your disabling condition interferes with your ability to perform that job.

Having short-term disability coverage is much less important than having long-term disability coverage for most people, especially if you have an adequate emergency fund or a dual-income household—though it certainly doesn't hurt to have it if you can get it at low cost or no cost through employment or otherwise.

Long-term disability coverage, on the other hand, is absolutely essential for almost everyone.

Long-term disability insurance is also what it sounds like: if you become disabled, whether that disability lasts for one year or the rest of your life, this policy will pay you a percentage of your lost income (again, usually around 60 percent) usually until age sixty-five. You will have to be initially certified as disabled by a doctor and then recertified periodically to continue receiving benefits. Most long-term disability policies have waiting periods (elimination periods) of at least ninety days before they will start paying benefits.

There are three main options for obtaining disability insurance: through an employer, through an affinity organization, or through private individual coverage.

If disability insurance is provided to you as an employee benefit, *take it.* A lot of large companies offer this as a standard benefit. In some cases, it's at no cost; in others, you can add it on to your existing benefits package at relatively low cost. I recommend having as much disability insurance as you can get, especially if it's as easy as filling out some paperwork with your employer.

> If your disability insurance premiums are paid for you by your employer, or you arrange to pay premiums with pre-tax dollars, your benefit payments will be taxable income for you. If you can arrange to pay your own premiums with after-tax dollars (which is easy to do with private/individual coverage), your benefit payments will not be taxable. I highly recommend finding a way to arrange for this, if possible.

If long-term disability insurance coverage isn't offered as a benefit through your employer, or if you're self-employed, you can still pursue coverage through one of the other two methods.

A lot of industry-related groups offer fairly affordable disability insurance policies to their members. For example, I have disability coverage through the National Association of Personal Financial Advisors. I recommend checking to see if your industry's affinity organization has a policy, and then becoming a member if they offer coverage.

Coverage provided to you through an employer or affinity organization is called group coverage. Meaning, usually, that the same standard disability policy covers all members of the group. These policies tend to be much cheaper than private/individual policies, but they also tend to terminate when you leave the employer or affinity organization. It's also possible to get group coverage in many cases with no medical underwriting.

Private or individual coverage is typically much more expensive but also highly customizable and will remain in place regardless of whether you change employers or leave an affinity organization. Private coverage is the gold standard of disability insurance. It's also quite expensive in most cases and requires medical underwriting for evidence of insurability. If your cash flows allow, I highly recommend that you consider private long-term disability coverage, which you can obtain by contacting an insurance broker.

LIFE INSURANCE

I get asked all the time, "How do you know if you need life insurance?"

My answer, as with disability insurance, is a simple one: if there's anyone you care about who would be financially worse off if you died tomorrow, then you should have life insurance.

If you're young, single, and have no children or other financial dependents—well, you probably don't need life insurance.

If you're coupled, but your partner is not financially dependent on you, then you likely don't need life insurance.

If, however, you have a mortgage with your partner or if you have children together, then you probably do.

For example: imagine a young married couple, we'll call them Jordan and Sam, with no children, no mortgage, and no joint debts. Jordan earns $200,000 a year and Sam earns $175,000. If Jordan died tomorrow, Sam would be okay financially, and vice versa. They probably don't need life insurance.

But let's say they buy a house and take on a $600,000 mortgage. In that case, they would both want at least some life insurance coverage—enough to help a surviving spouse pay the mortgage in case that one spouse died prematurely.

Now let's say that they have a child. Both of them need at least enough life insurance coverage to cover the mortgage *and* help the other cover the costs of raising their child as a single parent. This likely means enough to cover additional childcare, and perhaps money for education.

So, at a minimum, you should get enough coverage so that your financial dependents won't be left in the lurch financially should you die prematurely. One rule of thumb is that you should buy coverage to replace at least twenty (or more) years of your annual income.

Of course, at the end of the day, there is no cookie cutter formula for exactly how much coverage you need. That comes down to your specific financial situation and the needs of your financial dependents.

Term vs. Whole Life Insurance

There are two main types of life insurance: term and whole life (also called cash value insurance). Whole life insurance is appropriate for *almost* no one, but is widely and aggressively sold by unscrupulous salespeople masquerading as "financial advisors." Why? Because it's very expensive and therefore a great source of commissions for the people who sell it.

It's often pitched as a good investment or asset protection tool, but in most cases, it's a terrible investment and not suited for the average person's needs. Without getting into the weeds, I'll just say this: nearly everyone is better off with basic term life insurance. Don't let a "financial advisor" sell you whole life insurance.

Term insurance, on the other hand, is simply a death benefit. It's not an investment product, an asset protection tool, or anything else. When you buy term insurance, you pick a defined period of time (typically ten, twenty, or thirty years) during which your beneficiaries will be paid a certain sum of money, called a "death benefit," if you die. The cost of insurance usually comes down to the amount of death benefit you buy and your "insurability," i.e., how healthy you are.

My husband and I, for example, both just purchased twenty-year term life insurance policies. Having this coverage really helps us sleep at night, as we're a dual income household with a mortgage and a child on the way, and we live in an expensive city. We both wanted to have enough coverage for the other to be financially comfortable, and with plenty of school and childcare options, in case the other died prematurely. We're young and relatively healthy, so we're paying less than $1,200 per year for this coverage. The peace of mind is worth every penny!

Most people need both disability and life insurance while they are young. But your goal should be to accumulate enough assets to eventually "self-insure" for your own potential disability or premature death. This means that you eventually have enough money that you and your loved ones would not be *financially* worse off if you became disabled or died. When you do get to this point, you can drop your life and disability coverage.

WRAP UP

Remember Ben, from the beginning of this chapter? If he'd just had two basic insurance policies—umbrella liability and disability—his life would be in a far better place. Yes, he'd still be dealing with the physical fallout from the accident, but at least he'd still have his hard-earned nest egg and disability benefit payments to replace his lost income.

When I was creating this chapter, I worried that it was a bit too "all over the place"—after all, I threw in everything from car titling to life insurance. But each topic I've discussed in this chapter is one potential rope you can use to weave a safety net for yourself and your family.

What combination of "ropes" you need for your safety net depends on your particular needs and circumstances. My advice is to read this chapter so you know your options, and do some deep thinking about where your vulnerabilities lie. What holes can you plug *before* they become a problem?

Like I said, life can change in an instant. It's important to build wealth, but it's equally important to protect it.

LET'S BREAK IT DOWN

- A complete financial plan covers not only strategies for *building* wealth but also for *protecting* accumulated wealth from life's curveballs.
- Asset protection becomes increasingly important once you start to accumulate significant assets, but it's also important while you're early in the accumulation stage.
- When you are young, two of the worst things that can happen to you financially are for you to lose your ability to earn an income, or to have a significant monetary judgment entered against you. Unless you are already quite wealthy, financial setbacks like these can be very hard to recover from.
- Insurance is an incredibly powerful tool for risk management and asset protection, and in many cases, is the one thing preventing a life catastrophe from also becoming a financial catastrophe.
- Almost *everyone* needs some form(s) of insurance, to protect themselves, their loved ones, and their assets.

CONCLUSION

Remember Maggie, my Physician Assistant friend whom I introduced you to in the very beginning of this book? When we left off with her story, she and her husband Greg had just moved to Colorado for his dream job opportunity practicing environmental law. Once there, they found themselves in a tough spot. Maggie was temporarily out of work, and they had a second child on the way, a new mortgage, and over $300,000 in combined student loan debt.

But their story has a happy ending.

After having her second child, Maggie was able to find a good Physician Assistant job in Colorado. With her new income injecting some flexibility into her family's cash flows, she and Greg decided to sit down one weekend and do a full financial analysis of where they were and where they wanted to go. Together, they set two ambitious financial goals:

1. Have no debt other than their mortgage, in four years.
2. Have a combined net worth of at least $1 million within fifteen years.

No longer would they allow their debt to control their lives—they were going into attack mode.

They decided to continue living on only Greg's income, as they had while Maggie was out of work. They had already adjusted to it, and doing this allowed them to put every cent of Maggie's income entirely to paying off their student loans.

It's now been three years since they sat down and made this ambitious financial plan. When we caught up over the phone a few weeks ago, she told me that they were six months away from completely zeroing out their student loans. I asked her how they managed to do this, and she said, "We just act like I don't have an income."

They've also built a solid safety net. With umbrella liability insurance, uninsured motorist coverage, and life and disability coverage, they're well protected from financial disaster.

As they pay off more and more debt, they're also slowly starting to increase pre-tax salary deferrals into their 401(k)s.

They've become so used to living on one income that they don't plan to start spending Maggie's income once the student loans are wiped out. Instead, they plan to split her income into three buckets moving forward: college savings accounts for their kids, paying down their mortgage ahead of schedule, and saving for retirement.

This lifestyle might sound extreme, but they are happier and less stressed living on one income and attacking their loans than a lot of people I know who spend significantly more money on "enjoying life." Making measurable progress towards their goals has been very empowering and confidence-building for them. That confidence has led to even more conviction that they're capable of building wealth, which in turn has kept them solidly on the path there. It's a self-fulfilling cycle.

Contrary to what many would assume, this lifestyle does not leave them feeling deprived; it leaves them feeling completely fulfilled.

And they don't live like hermits either. They eat out, travel, and live in a nice house, as Greg's income allows. But they could easily live "bigger" and spend much more if they didn't make the choice to live on one income.

Every year, Maggie and Greg take a weekend away, just the two of them. They leave the kids with relatives, head to a resort, and use that time to talk about their financial plan for the year ahead. They make a list of goals, discuss how to achieve them, review their cash flows and net worth, and prioritize what to focus on for the upcoming twelve months until they do it again. They talk about everything; nothing is off limits.

Consistently setting goals and tracking progress in this way has allowed them to remain disciplined and on track. They will likely reach financial independence well before "normal" retirement age.

And in the meantime, they're getting to live the lives they want—happy, stable, and full of family, fun, and freedom.

SPENDING VS. QUALITY OF LIFE

Many studies have been done about how much money we truly need to be happy. We've all heard that money can't buy happiness...but can it help?

One highly publicized study, using data from the Gallup World Poll, a survey of 1.7 million people from 164 countries, found that $75,000 is the income sweet spot for individual happiness. More specifically, the analysis found that earning between $60,000 and $75,000 was the optimal income for an individual's emotional well-being, and $95,000 was the optimal salary for an individual's "life satisfaction," which takes into account long-term goals and other macro considerations.

In fact, the study found, increases in reported life satisfaction essentially stopped at that $95,000 mark. Beyond that, making more had no meaningful effect on happiness.[15]

I've seen the powerful truth of this, both in my own life and in the lives of the people I work with. Once you are making enough to be comfortable and have basic financial stability—enough to afford some of the "wants" instead of just the needs—making more doesn't really move the needle on long-term happiness.

Scientists think this is due to hedonic adaptation—our human tendency to revert back to our mean level of happiness relatively quickly after deviations up and down from it.

As it turns out, good things don't make us any happier than we usually are, at least not for long—but bad things don't make us feel worse for long either.

A well-known study on this topic from the 1970s studied both lottery winners and recent paraplegics to determine the effects of their recent fates upon their subjective happiness. Researchers then followed up again a decade later and found

15 Jamie Ducharme, "This Is the Amount of Money You Need to Be Happy, According to Research," Money.com, February 14, 2018, https://money.com/ideal-income-study/.

that both groups had reverted to being more or less as happy as they had been before their accidents or financial windfalls.

So what's the point of all this?

Before you spend money on something, ask yourself why you want to buy it—and be honest with yourself. If you're buying it because you think it will make you happier, something we all want, the reality is that it probably won't have the desired effect, at least not for long. Think back to past purchases—especially those you couldn't technically afford, or for which the money could have been put to better use—and ask yourself, "Did that really make me happy for any meaningful period of time? *Was it worth it?*"

Rather than thinking of money as a tool you can use to buy *things*, think of it as a tool that can give you options and freedom, independence and peace of mind. *Those* are things that having money can provide you that almost certainly will increase your long-term happiness and well-being.

NOW WHAT?

From here, I recommend that you go back to chapter 2, and start building your plan for reaching financial independence by working through the five-step Personal Financial Audit process:

1. Confront reality.
2. Educate yourself.
3. Set goals.
4. Make a plan to achieve them.
5. Reevaluate and track your progress.

Look through the action steps at the end of each chapter and incorporate those details into your plan—starting with the specific goals/steps you can put in place immediately and making notes for the ones you want to add in later.

Most importantly, *write it down.* Do more research if you need to, whether on your own financial situation or about a particular subject area that is interesting to you. Set calendar appointments for tracking your progress and schedule time, whether monthly, quarterly, or annually, to reevaluate how far you've come and reprioritize as you check off your initial goals.

Your plan will change and evolve as your life does.

PARTING WORDS

Remember that you are young. Time is on your side, and that's an extremely powerful tool for building wealth if you use it wisely.

If you're reading this book, you've already taken the first

step on the path to financial independence, and you're well ahead of most of your peers. So don't stop here, keep going. Build momentum, and you'll be well on your way to having independence, peace of mind, and control over how you spend your time and money.

It's your life—go live it.

ABOUT THE AUTHOR

RACHEL PODNOS O'LEARY is a CERTIFIED FINANCIAL PLANNER™ with Wealth Care LLC. She earned both a bachelor's degree and a law degree from the University of Florida, where she was also an enthusiastic Gator cheerleader. Following law school, Rachel became a member of the Florida Bar and later became a fee-only financial planner. She currently lives in Washington, D.C., with her husband and daughter.